Marriage in Men's Lives

Marriage in Men's Lives

STEVEN L. NOCK

New York   Oxford
Oxford University Press
1998

Oxford University Press

Oxford   New York

Athens   Auckland   Bangkok   Bogota   Bombay
Buenos Aires   Calcutta   Cape Town   Dar es Salaam
Delhi   Florence   Hong Kong   Istanbul   Karachi
Kuala Lumpur   Madras   Madrid   Melbourne
Mexico City   Nairobi   Paris   Singapore
Taipei   Tokyo   Toronto   Warsaw

and associated companies in
Berlin   Ibadan

Library of Congress Cataloging-in-Publication Data
Nock, Steven L.
Marriage in men's lives / Steven L. Nock.
p.   cm.
Includes bibliographical references and index.
ISBN 0-19-512056-6
1. Men—United States—Attitudes.   2. Men—United States—Psychology.
3. Husbands—United States—Attitudes.   4. Husbands—United States—Psychology.
5. Masculinity—United States.   6. Marriage—United States.   I. Title.
HQ1090.3.N63   1998
305.31—dc21   98-21949

9 8 7 6 5 4 3 2 1

Printed in the United States of America
on acid-free paper

To my wife, Daphne, for the marriage we share

Acknowledgments

I have been the lucky beneficiary of help from many people in the course of conducting the research reported in this book. Many colleagues at the University of Virginia offered help with methods, logic, and arguments. Chuck Denk, Steve Patterson, and Steve Finkel gave valuable assistance on statistical matters and methods of analysis. Tim Tolson and Doug Lloyd managed to keep my computer running despite the enormous demands made on it.

To my friend and colleague, E. Mavis Hetherington, I offer my most sincere thanks for the many lunches we shared to discuss the ideas in this work. Our conversations and friendship sustained me throughout the project. Margaret Brinig, Paul Kingston, and Steve Rhodes read the entire manuscript at various stages and offered advice and suggestions. Elizabeth Scott at the University of Virginia Law School provided needed guidance in my study of family law and read several chapters of the manuscript. Susan McKinnon and Ellen Contini Morava guided my search of materials in cultural anthropology.

Colleagues elsewhere were equally generous in their help. Suzanne Bianchi at the University of Maryland offered advice on the design of the research. Diane Hansen at the Center for Demography and Ecology at the University of Wisconsin gave assistance with the acquisition and analysis of the National Survey of Families and Households. Steve McClosky at the Center for Human Resource Research at the Ohio State University guided me through the acquisition and analysis of the National Longitudinal Survey of Youth. William Marsiglio at the University of Florida offered suggestions about fatherhood as an element of marriage. Alan Booth and Nan Crouter gave me the chance to present some of the earliest results when they invited me to participate in the Men in Families Conference at Pennsylvania State University.

This work staddles several academic disciplines beyond my own (sociology), including law, anthropology, and psychology. I count myself lucky to have generous colleagues here, and elsewhere, willing to offer assistance to a novice in their fields.

To my friends at Oxford University Press who helped create and produce this book, I offer my sincere thanks. Joan Bossert, Executive Editor, offered valuable advice on almost every page of the manuscript. And special thanks to Will Moore who supervised the production. Together, we learned about the problems of using graphs produced by statistical software. He solved them with admirable patience and creativity.

My most profound debt is to my wife, Daphne, to whom this book is dedicated. She discussed the thesis on countless occasions, read every draft, offered detailed comments and criticisms, and retained her sense of humor about a husband explaining why he benefits so enormously from his marriage to her.

Contents

Marriage in Men's Lives

Introduction

My goal in this book is to answer two questions: *How* and *why* does marriage change men? The many beneficial effects of marriage are well-known. Married people are generally healthier; they live longer, earn more, have better mental health and better sex lives, and are happier than their unmarried counterparts. Further, married individuals have lower rates of suicide, fatal accidents, acute and chronic illnesses, alcoholism, and depression than other people (Crago, 1972; Crum, Helzer, and Anthony, 1993; Ernster, Sacks, Selvin, and Petrakis, 1979; Layne and Whitehead, 1985; Lillenfield, Levin, and Kessler, 1972; Lynch, 1977; Metropolitan Life Insurance Company, 1957; Morowitz, 1975; Pearlin and Johnson, 1977; Smith, Mercy, and Conn, 1988; Stack, 1992; Verbrugge, 1979; see Waite, 1995, for a review). Some disagreement may exist about the magnitude of such effects, but they are almost certainly the result of marriage, rather than self-selection. Married people do not simply *appear* to be better off than unmarried people; rather, marriage changes people in ways that produce such benefits (Coombs, 1991).

Even though marriage contributes to the well-being of both men and women, husbands are the greater beneficiaries. Men reap greater gains than women for virtually every outcome affected by marriage. When women benefit from marriage, it is because they are in a satisfying relationship; but men appear much less sensitive to the quality of their marriages and gain by simply *being married* (Gove, Hughes, and Style, 1983). Marriage itself improves men's lives; the quality of the marriage affects women's lives.

When I began this project my intention was to explain how and why marriage changes men and women. In the course of the research, however, I realized that marriage has different effects for men and women because it is a very different experience for each gender. Husbands and wives experience their marriages differently because the cultural definition of what it means to be a married person is different for men and women (Bernard, 1982: 9). Both genders benefit from marriage but for different reasons. Thus, *Marriage in Men's Lives* is the first of two projects. The next will consider marriage in women's lives.

What is it about being married that matters for men? And why would the *qual-*

ity of the relationship be less important for husbands than for wives? The answer to both of these questions, I believe, is that marriage is a social institution. That means conventional expectations are associated with it—customary ways to be a good husband. In this sense a man does more than simply marry a woman. He also binds himself to a system of rules, some quite formal and some little more than conventional expectations. As a husband, a man becomes the subject of others' expectations and will be expected to do things differently than he did as a bachelor. When children are born, others automatically assume he is the father, and his responsibilities and obligations to his children will begin immediately. As a husband and as a father, he will be treated differently. No matter what a marriage may mean to a particular man and his wife, the fact that a man is a husband carries great significance to others. This means that in the search for how and why marriage matters to men, marriage emerges as much more than a relationship between two partners. It also is a relationship defined by cultural assumptions. By their marriages, husbands and wives accept an obligation to be faithful, to give and receive help in times of sickness, and to endure hardships. Not everyone will be able to remain true to such vows. However, it is more difficult for a married than for an unmarried person to break such promises *because* they are part of our laws, religions, and definitions of morality. Others have taken identical vows throughout history. Collectively, society enforces these ideals both formally and informally. Nothing of the sort can be said about any other type of intimate relationship between two adults. Understanding this helps us make sense of why marriage changes men.

My own research (as well as that of many others) has shown, for example, that couples in long-term cohabiting relationships differ in predictable ways from married couples. The cohabiting couple is united by bonds of love and affection, but very little else. Such individuals have more freedom than their married counterparts. No formal laws and few informal norms dictate the terms of the cohabiting relationship. There are no conventional assumptions about how people who are living together should behave. But such freedom comes with a cost. Cohabiting couples are less satisfied than married spouses with their partnerships, are not as close to their parents, are less committed to each other, and, if they eventually marry, have higher chances of divorce (Nock, 1995b).

The ubiquity of marriage suggests how highly it is valued by Americans. In 1995, 9 in 10 (92.3%) individuals older than 35 had married at least once. The U.S. Census Bureau projects similarly high rates of marriage until 2010, when 91% of Americans >35 will have married (U.S. Bureau of the Census, 1996b). The overall percentage of adults expected to ever marry may have dropped somewhat in recent years, but the decline has been from about 95% to about 90% (U.S. Bureau of the Census, 1992b). Even those who divorce remarry at very high rates. Indeed, remarriage is so common that half (46.3%) of all marriages involve at least one previously married person (National Center for Health Statistics, 1995: Table 6). Current national estimates show that between two-thirds and three-fourths of divorced persons remarry (Bumpass, Sweet, and Castro Martin, 1990; U.S. Bureau of the Census 1992b: 5).

Despite our high regard for marriage and high marriage rates, there is a widespread belief that American marriages are weak and troubled. Two-thirds (66%) of American adults believe that couples do not take marriage seriously enough when divorce is easily available. And only half (53%) of Americans believe that married people are generally happier than unmarried persons (General Social Surveys, 1994). Even though divorce rates have remained stable since the late 1980s, the current levels are higher than in any prior historical period (National Center for Health Statistics, 1995: Figure 2). How can marriage be so good for people when they perceive it to be so bad?

In fact, marriages are not that bad. Individual spouses may focus on their personal relationships with one another and with children. But every marriage is much more than the sum of such associations. Even for the troubled partner whose private married life is unhappy, there are potential benefits to being married. These benefits accrue from others' assumptions about married people and treatment of them. Marriage, despite the details of intimate life, is part of an identity. A husband is a married man regardless of the quality of his marriage. To understand this aspect of marriage means that one must focus on the public rather than the private dimensions—on what is expected of men *because* they are husbands.

My first task, therefore, is to develop a definition of marriage as a social institution. I identify those dimensions of marriage about which there is very strong consensus. I rely on three diverse sources to assess consensus. First is domestic relations law, including appellate cases from state and federal courts. The law is a conservative statement of our collective ideals and embodies our beliefs about how things should be. The second source is public opinion surveys. Large nationally representative surveys of adults have been conducted repeatedly for three decades. The surveys I use provide a glimpse into what Americans think about important social and personal issues. Overwhelming agreement about some statement or question about marriage in the General Social Surveys, the National Longitudinal Survey of Youth, the National Survey of Families and Households, the National Health and Social Life Survey, or other national surveys consulted for this project may be taken as evidence of consensus among Americans on a particular issue. Finally, religious doctrine, especially the Bible, is the third source. Marriage is a core ritual in all religious traditions. Most marriages are conducted by religious officials; very few Americans claim to have *no* religious affiliation. The traditional, well-known ceremonial vows (e.g., for better or worse, in sickness and in health, until death us do part, etc.) are part of our collective understanding of the institution. Not surprisingly, my study of these diverse sources revealed similar definitions of marriage. Any other result would have been quite remarkable because marriage is such a central element of our culture.

Americans generally agree about six dimensions of marriage. Together, these constitute a *normative definition* of marriage. They are ideals that define what marriages *should* be:

1. Marriage is a free personal choice, based on love.
2. Maturity is a presumed requirement for marriage.
3. Marriage is a heterosexual relationship.
4. The husband is the head, and principal earner, in a marriage.
5. Sexual fidelity and monogamy are expectations for marriage.
6. Marriage typically involves children.

Not all married couples conform to such canons, and not all wish to. Still, these dimensions are a statement of how marriage is understood in America. My attempt to understand how and why marriage changes men relies on these core elements of the institution and inform my theory about how and why each one matters to husbands.

This traditional model of marriage also assumes a husband who supports his wife and children. Few acceptable alternatives exist for married men. Even though a majority of wives are gainfully employed and contribute economically to their families, virtually all working-age husbands are employed. To be a married man in America means that a husband is expected to be engaged in the business of earning a living. The husband who cannot do so may be pitied. But the husband who *will not* work is scorned. This simple commonplace observation contains the key to understanding much about marriage in men's lives.

That key is the connection between marriage and conventional ideas about masculinity. Historically, masculinity has implied three things about a man: he should be the father of his wife's children, he should be the provider for his wife and children, and he should protect his family. Accordingly, the male who refused to provide for or protect his family was not only a bad husband, he was somehow less than a man. In marriage, men do those things that are culturally accepted as basic elements of adult masculinity. This is the central theme of *Marriage in Men's Lives*: marriage changes men because it is the venue in which adult masculinity is developed and sustained. Normative marriage, as outlined above, requires and venerates behaviors that are central to cultural definitions of manhood.

Does this mean that men are forced to accept a particular model of marriage? After all, husbands and wives have great discretion about how to arrange their intimate lives. But the simple fact is that most men and women organize their married lives in broad accord with the outlines of normative marriage. My explanation is that normative marriage is the only way by which *most* males can become "men." Once this basic premise is understood, it becomes much easier to understand why marriage has positive effects for men.

I suggest that masculinity is precarious and must be sustained in adulthood. Normative marriage does this. A man develops, sustains, and displays his masculine identity in his marriage. The adult roles that men occupy as husbands are core aspects of their masculinity. I believe this is a clue to why marriage is beneficial in men's lives.

Cultures differ in how they recognize and foster masculinity. In some, elaborate rites of passage mark the transitions from one stage of boyhood to another along the route to eventual adult masculinity. In others, such as our own, however, there are few public markers. At what point is a young male a man? And how do we know? In the absence of ritualized transitions or other clearly defined points in the life course that establish the attainment of mature adulthood for a man, attention shifts to marriage. As I will argue, marriage is a *rite of passage into manhood*. Once married, a man is a different social and legal person and is held to different standards and accorded different treatment by others.

In marriage, a man will find the means necessary to develop and sustain his masculinity. The dimensions of normative marriage are powerful symbols and tools for doing the things expected of men *as men*. As fathers, providers, and protectors, married men are expected to differ from unmarried men in their legitimate outlets for *adult achievement*, in their involvement, participation, and *engagement in social life*, and in their expressions of *generosity or philanthropy*. Each of these will be shown to be a component of masculine gender in American society. Many are related to basic cultural standards of *providing for* and *protecting* others. Some are related to methods of *displaying* gender. All, however, are integral components of masculinity.

Moreover, men arrange much of their lives in accordance with expectations of them *as husbands*. The traits expected of married men *as husbands* are the same traits expected of husbands *as men*—responsibility (for wife and children), maturity, and fidelity. In this sense, marriage is a metaphor for much else in men's lives. Married men are more productive and achieve more than bachelors. They depend less on others. Marriage changes the nature of men's engagement with others. Friendships and contacts with friends change, as do organizational memberships and allegiances. And patterns of help and generosity are transformed. As a husband, a man is expected to be an active, independent provider who lives in a world of objective and often impersonal rules. Married men's relationships with others are not created so much as they are *joined*. Little effort is required to establish them. Instead, they require that men conform to the accepted standards that apply to them as members or incumbents of social roles.

Once married, men are more likely to become *members* of a church and less likely to spend time with friends. Once married, men often drop their involvements in informal groups in favor of more formal organizations. Men are more likely to spend time with their relatives once they are married. In all such endeavors, husbands are bound to relationships with others by virtue of their membership in an organization or in a kinship group. In each, well-defined standards determine acceptable and unacceptable behavior. The married men in this research resemble those described by Carol Gilligan: "Relationships [for men] are often cast in the language of achievement, characterized by their success or failure. . . . Instead of attachment, individual achievement rivets the male imagination" (1982: 154,163).

Men can judge themselves as good or bad husbands because the standards of normative marriage are also well-known. Good husbands are mature, faithful, generous fathers and providers. Good husbands are expected to achieve, to help others, and to remain true to their promises. Good husbands are good men.

Does this mean that the traditional male-dominated form of marriage is better than more egalitarian models? Do these results imply that equality in marriage is undesirable? And, most critically, do the results of this analysis imply that contemporary, less traditional models of marriage and living arrangements are undesirable? These have been the most challenging questions in this project. Some readers will interpret this book as a strong rationale for every aspect of traditional marriages. Some will construe the results as an indictment of the goals of modern feminism. Indeed, much in the following analyses shows "traditional" marriage patterns to be quite beneficial for men. But this is not a criticism of gender equality, and the findings should not strike anyone as surprising. Marriage has historically been organized to men's advantage. The news in this book is about how and why that arrangement matters for men. Once this is understood, I believe it will be easier to understand how and why the prevailing model of normative marriage is changing, as it must.

The basic research strategy used throughout this project relies on two types of comparisons. First, I assess men before and after they get married to see how various dimensions of their lives change in the interim. Here the question is whether marriage creates predictable changes in men's lives. Second, I follow these married men as they experience changes in the basic dimensions of normative marriage. For example, over the course of several years, children are born or leave home, wives enter the labor force or leave it, and incomes rise or fall. Each dimension of normative marriage is measured by an indicator of this type. The question is whether there are predictable changes in men's lives when there are changes in the normative dimensions of their marriages. Throughout, I focus on three aspects of men's lives suggested by the theory: adult achievement (e.g., income, weeks worked), social participation (e.g., church attendance, membership in organizations), and generosity (gifts of money or kind to relatives, friends, or others).

The results are consistent with the theory. Marriage brings about predictable changes in all dimensions studied. Once married, men earn more, work more, and achieve more. Once married, men see less of their friends and drop memberships in relatively unstructured types of organizations (e.g., health clubs). They are more likely to participate in organized, formal relationships governed by clear standards of performance and membership (e.g., church). And, once married, men are less likely to contribute money or assistance to individuals they are not related to by blood or marriage. Moreover, when men's marriages change toward more normative patterns, there are comparable shifts of the sort just described.

American marriages are slowly changing in consistent ways. Most generally, what it means to be a married woman today is very different from what it was in the recent past. Increasing rates of female labor-force involvement, delayed marriage, reduced fertility, and higher chances of divorce all require changes that signal a departure from some aspects of normative marriage. These changes have significant implications for men and women. But the biggest challenges in the future will confront men. The battles for greater equality and opportunities for women have been (and continue to be) waged openly in law, the economy, education, religion, and politics. Strangely, the basic institution of marriage has not yet been redefined to accommodate the significantly changed lives of most women. Americans have not, as yet, arrived at a common definition of marriage based on extensive dependencies that accommodate the greater gender equality found elsewhere in society. It is quite clear, however, that we must. All social institutions are integrated affairs. It is not possible to have profound changes in one or two without corresponding changes in all others. To the extent that our public lives have been changed by transformations in ideas about men and women, then our private lives must also change. Indeed, many of the problems faced by contemporary families result from new ways of thinking that originated in these public institutions—in the economy or in schools, for example. Those problems are best seen as the cost we are paying to bridge the gulf between our family lives and our public lives. The idea of what it means to be married and to have a family will change, albeit slowly, as all other institutions change.

Marriage in Men's Lives suggests how these changes might occur. As marriages become less traditional, there are profound implications for men because the institutional framework of matrimony is largely organized around traditional assumptions about husbands. However, husbands and wives are becoming more equal because both partners increasingly depend on one another's incomes. The contemporary married couple typically includes two earners. But the power imbalances that are part of the assumption that husbands are the heads of their families may be inconsistent with this pattern. The challenge is to recast the institution as one in which pervasive dependencies exist without inequity. Without dependency, there is little to bind couples together, except their love and mutual affection. Studies of cohabiting couples show that such glue is weak and destabilizes the entire arrangement. Therefore, complete equality in all matters cannot sustain enduring marriages. Something else is needed. I propose it is an institutional framework, or model, of marriage that casts husbands and wives in *mutually dependent* roles.

The newly emerging model of marriage is similar in many respects to the normative model already outlined. Most dimensions of traditional marriage are intact and will probably remain so. The greatest change is that dependencies in marriage are equalizing. The normative expectation for a married man is that he must provide for his wife and children. This means that wives and children are *dependents*. But it is no longer true that husbands are expected to do *all* the providing. That task is now partly shared, and, undoubtedly, provider roles will continue to expand among wives.

This does not abolish the wife's dependence on her husband. But it does mean that husbands depend on their wives. Married couples are defining marriage as an arrangement that depends on the combined resources generated by both partners. For the vast majority of people, neither husband nor wife alone is able to afford any other arrangement. In this sense, Americans are returning to a *more traditional* form of marriage. The typical marriage in the first half of the twentieth century was an unusual one. The arrangement in which husbands were responsible for the entire family economy was an historical aberration that lasted only about half a century. Until the turn of this century, and since about 1970, most married couples relied on a combination of economic efforts by both spouses to keep the household going. Contemporary marriages will more closely resemble earlier arrangements than those of the early twentieth century. Such marriages will still require that husbands provide for wives and children. But they also will require that wives provide for husbands and children.

The changes we are beginning to see in the institution of marriage do not portend the end of gendered marriages. But they probably do mean the end of many of the invidious inequalities based on gender in marriage. The model of marriage now emerging will be good for men, just as the traditional model was. But the new model of marriage will be better for women than the traditional one was.

Marriage is probably the last basic social institution to change as a result of new ideas about what it means to be a man or a woman. My hope is that *Marriage in Men's Lives* will offer a perspective on the implications of these changes.

◆ 2 ◆

Marriage as a Social Institution

A marriage is much more than the sum of two spouses. It is also a relationship defined by legal, moral, and conventional assumptions. While one can imagine a variety of close personal affiliations uniting two adults, the variety of marriage affiliations is much narrower because marriage is an *institution*, culturally patterned and integrated into other basic social institutions, such as education, the economy, and politics. Marriage has rules that originate outside any particular union of two spouses and that establish *soft boundaries* around the relationship that influence the partners in many ways. The boundaries around marriages are the commonly understood allowable limits of behavior that distinguish marriage from all other kinds of relationships. The social norms that define the institution of marriage identify married spouses in ways that distinguish them from others. Married couples have something that other couples lack: they are heirs to a vast system of understood principles that help organize and sustain their lives.

One explanation for how marriage matters to men is that it provides structure to their lives and organizes their ambitions. This is an old argument, first suggested a century ago by Emile Durkheim, who demonstrated the protective role of marriage in preventing suicide. Durkheim observed that since basic human necessities (food, housing, clothing) are more or less available in all advanced societies, desires among modern humans are focused on well-being, comfort, luxury, and prestige. Sooner or later, however, the appetite for such rewards becomes sated. One of the central problems in modern society, therefore, is establishing legitimate boundaries around such desires. This, Durkheim believed, can be accomplished only by social institutions such as marriage (1951: 247–49).

Durkheim explained the function of marriage for men by noting how unrestrained longings and desires must be checked. Marriage benefits men, Durkheim believed, because, as an organ of society, it restrains their otherwise uncontrollable impulses. Discussing such desires and impulses, Durkheim observed:

> By forcing a man to attach himself forever to the same woman, marriage assigns
> a strictly definite object to the need for love, and closes the horizon. This deter-

mination is what forms the state of moral equilibrium from which the husband benefits. Being unable to seek other satisfactions than those permitted, without transgressing his duty, he restricts his desires to them. The salutary discipline to which he is subjected makes it his duty to find his happiness in his lot, and by doing so supplies him with the means. (1951: 270–71)

Two people may enjoy a harmonious and happy life without the benefit of marriage. In fact, growing numbers of Americans appear to believe that unmarried *cohabitation* offers something that marriage does not: freedom from the rules of marriage because there are no widely accepted and approved boundaries around cohabitation. Unmarried partners have tremendous freedom to decide how they will arrange their relationships. Each partner must decide how to deal with the other's parents, for example. Couples must decide whether vacations will be taken together or separately. Money may be pooled or held in separate accounts. And the parents of a cohabiting couple will also need to create a relationship with them with little guidance. Is the cohabiting couple to be treated as a married pair? In such small ways, cohabiting couples and their associates must create their relationship. Married couples may also face decisions about some of these matters. However, married spouses have a pattern to follow. For most matters of domestic life, marriage supplies a template—what cohabiting couples lack. They are exempt from the vast range of marriage norms and laws in our society.

A man can say to his spouse: "I am your husband. You are my wife. I am expected to do certain things for you, and you likewise. We have pledged our faithfulness. We have sworn to forego others. We have made a commitment to our children. We have a responsibility and obligation to our close relatives, as they have to us." These statements are not simply personal pledges. They are also enforceable. Others will expect these things of the couple. Laws, religion, and customs bolster this contract. When this man says to someone, "I would like you to meet my wife," this simple declaration says a great deal.

Consider an unmarried couple living happily together. What, if any, are the conventional assumptions that can be made? What are the limits to behavior? To whom is each obligated? Whom can this couple count on for help in times of need? And how do you complete this introduction of one's cohabiting partner: "I would like you to meet my . . ."? The lack of a word for such a partner clearly indicates how little such relationships are governed by convention. Alternatively, we may say that such a relationship is *not* an institution.

Marriage is a form of "capital" just as surely as any other resource. "If physical capital is wholly tangible, being embodied in observable material form, and human capital is less tangible, being embodied in skills and knowledge acquired by an individual, *social capital* is less tangible yet, for it exists in the *relations* among persons. Just as physical capital and human capital facilitate productive activity, social capital does as well" (Coleman, 1988: S100–S101). Social capital consists of extensive networks of individuals linked by bonds of trustworthiness and trust.

This type of capital is produced in relationships predicated on the belief (i.e., trust) that obligations will be incurred *and* repaid. Through their marriages, husbands and wives become connected to new kin (and friends of new kin). Kinship ties forged through marriage differ from those in more casual relationships. Such relationships are extensively woven with threads of obligations. In times of need, one may call upon relatives and expect assistance. The enduring nature of kinship obligations means that such debts persist and bind relatives together in an ongoing relationship.

Social capital also embeds individuals in networks that channel valued knowledge and information among all members. Such networks are sustained by social norms and social sanctions (honor, status, etc.) that facilitate certain actions and constrain others. Individuals benefit just as much from the accumulation of social capital as from other types of capital. Yet social capital cannot be separated from the configuration of institutions and communities (other people) that give it meaning and consequence. In short, the institution of marriage is an individual asset. Although intangible, it is no less important than other assets, yet more difficult to sustain (or accumulate) because it exists only *as* relationships with others.

The soft boundaries of marriage distinguish it qualitatively from all other forms of relationships. Therefore, to understand how marriage affects spouses, one must consider the various rules that define it. Thus, it would be well to reemphasize here the six dimensions that define normative marriage in America: marriages are entered *voluntarily* by *mature, heterosexual* adults with the expectation that husbands will be the *principal earners,* that both partners will be *sexually faithful,* and that married partners will become *parents.* Although many marriages depart from these ideals, the ideals still constitute the core of normative marriage as it is expressed in law, religion, and custom. Normative marriage is a form of social control, a way by which behaviors and aspirations are channeled appropriately. It is a force greater than the individuals involved because it represents the collective sentiments of others. Marriage in this view is qualitatively different from other intimate relationships. Much of the meaning of marriage in men's lives will be found in these rules. Together, these six premises provide a definition of marriage that will inform the rest of this work. As I will show, these normative expectations are the reason for the beneficial consequences of marriage for men.

The Meaning of Marriage for Men

One of the most firmly established and replicable findings in social science is that married people are healthier than unmarried ones. On a wide range of indicators of psychological well-being, married people generally fare better. At first glance, such a finding makes sense. After all, divorce and widowhood are both very distressing events. However, even never-married adults perform less ably, psychologically and physically, than those who are married (see Mirowsky and Ross, 1989, for a review).

The *psychological benefits* of marriage, however, are not easily explained. For example, the simple presence of others in the household might reasonably foster a sense of belonging, security, and comfort that buffers the effects of stressful events. In the absence of others in one's domestic life, loneliness and isolation could account for singles' typically poorer profiles. However, this is not the case. Research comparing various types of unmarried persons (never married, divorced or separated, and widowed) according to whether they lived alone showed that living alone, per se, is not associated with higher levels of distress. In fact, those who live alone and those who live with relatives or friends have similar distress levels. The difference in distress is between married people and everyone else (Hughes and Gove, 1981).

Though provocative, such findings have been refined by the discovery that bad marriages do not *always* appear to be appreciably better than no marriage at all. In fact, people who describe their marriages as unhappy more closely resemble unmarried than married individuals in their well-being. However, marital happiness is much more important for women than for men in terms of mental health. "When we compare the strength of the relationship between marital happiness and mental health, it is very clear that the relationship is stronger for married females than for married males. . . . Thus, marital status is more important for males than for females while the affective quality of marriage is more important for females than for males" (Gove, Hughes, and Style, 1983: 128).

In short, just being married appears to be more beneficial to men than to women, whereas the *quality* of the actual marriage appears more important to wives than to husbands. Why men are less responsive to the overall quality of their marriages than to the status of being married has not been explained. Yet this finding bears repeating because it highlights an important quality of marriage in men's lives. Marriage is typically an asset for men, regardless of the quality of the marital union.

Marriage is also good for *physical health*, especially men's. Men appear to reap the most physical health benefits from marriage and suffer the greatest health consequences when they divorce (Reissman and Gerstel, 1985). Demographers Hu and Goldman (1990) showed that the excess mortality rates (higher than predicted by age) of unmarried men (relative to married men) exceed those of unmarried women in 16 countries. Mortality for unmarried men is twice that of their married counterparts (1.5 times greater for unmarried than married women). Married men have lower rates of heavy drinking and alcohol dependency than divorced, widowed, or never married males (Crum, Helzer, and Anthony, 1993; Layne and Whitehead, 1985). The health correlates or consequences of marriage consistently differ for men and women, with men appearing to benefit more than women.

There are several possible reasons for such findings. First, and most obviously, marriage is a selective process. Not every person who wishes to marry actually does so. It is possible that men who exhibit various symptoms of mental health problems or other undesirable traits are less likely to get married than healthier, more successful men. These problems thus would make the population of unmarried men appear to be less healthy. Busy married men may be less likely to miss work, visit a doctor, be hospitalized, or utilize other types of health care. Lower use rates imply that married men are healthier, but in fact they simply use health care less often (Gotlib and McCabe, 1990; Verbrugge, 1979).

Alternatively, marriage may actually *cause* the differences found in comparisons of married and unmarried men. Marriage involves a lifestyle different from bachelorhood. Wives are important sources of help and assistance to their husbands. Men may be encouraged by wives to break bad habits, attend to their health, and so on. The greater social involvement of married persons may mediate some types of mental health problems by providing networks of support (Waite, 1995).

Before I attempt to identify the *beneficial* elements of marriage in men's lives, consider how it might affect men overall. Here I consider only aspects actually unique to marriage, not generic factors of all intimate relationships.

In the most general sense, the difference between marriage and other forms of intimate relationships is that marriage begins with a template supplied by the culture. "Marriage seems to lead its own separate existence, quite apart from particular married couples" (Skolnick, 1992: 280). The definition of normative marriage (monogamy, fidelity, etc.) provides a clue to the possible dimensions of marriage that might influence individual men, yet it does not adequately explain how such things matter. How, for example, might the norm of fidelity matter to a man? Or the expectation that husbands be fathers?

Challenges to Normative Marriage

One way to identify how normative marriage matters to men is to consider widespread attempts to *change* it. Challenges to traditional marriage provide a clue to certain problematic aspects. Whether they constitute actual problems is not the concern. Rather, such challenges identify particularly significant dimensions of marriage that matter to large numbers of people.

Cohabitation

One challenge that deserves special attention is the growing practice of unmarried cohabitation. Presumably, many of the intimate aspects of the two relationships may be the same, yet only one is socially defined. If there are consistent differences between the two types of relationships, they reflect the force of normative patterns.

An impressive amount of research has been conducted on cohabitation. Since many such unions are precursors to marriage and last but a few months, it is important to restrict the focus to cohabitation and marriages of comparable length to draw comparisons. Such a comparison shows that marriage is likely to produce greater commitment to partners than cohabitation because such commitments are enforced. They are difficult to abrogate (divorce is required to end the relationship and child-support endures even after a divorce). In a large national sample of individuals and couples, married people expressed higher levels of commitment to partners than comparable cohabiting individuals. This means that the perceived consequences of ending the relationship are greater for married than for cohabiting couples. And this difference is important in explaining cohabiting couples' reported poorer quality of the relationship overall. In short, marriage is associated with greater commitment than is cohabitation (Nock, 1995b). Cohabiting individuals also appear less committed to the *idea* of legal marriage (Thompson and Colela, 1992).

Unmarried couples living together are more insistent on *equality* in partners' economic contributions. Married couples, on the other hand, are more oriented to an economic division of labor in which one spouse earns most of the income. Cohabitation thus differs from marriage in terms of gender-related division of labor in the union. Married couples with an employed wife, for example, are *more likely* to divorce than those in which the wife is not employed. Among cohabitors, however, unions are *less likely* to end when both partners work for pay and their earnings are more equal (Brines and Joyner, 1993). These differences are also reflected in opinion research. Cohabiting couples are more likely than married partners to believe that men and women should share equally in household chores, even while they tend to perform such tasks like married couples do (i.e., tasks are gender-specific, Macklin, 1983). Finally, cohabiting couples are less committed to permanence. Half of cohabiting relationships end in fewer than two years (resulting either in marriage or a break-up), and almost all such relationships end before five years (Bumpass and Sweet, 1989; Thornton, 1988).

Cohabitation differs from marriage in predictable ways that reflect differences in institutionalization. Cohabitation is associated with lower levels of commitment to partners and to the relationship, with a correspondingly higher rate of dissolution. Gender equality is more highly valued. Such findings suggest that marriage represents a more enduring relationship based on dependence and commitment. Moreover, gender has differing meanings in the two relationships, especially as this central issue involves division of responsibilities and equality between partners.

Provider Role

When attention turns to criticisms of specific aspects of normative marriage, to attempts to modify the traditional relationship, and to rejections of certain elements of it, clues to how normative marriage is experienced are found. Indeed, such a review reveals the *central role* that gender plays in marriage. More particularly, it shows how the traditional assignment of tasks and responsibilities based on sex has been a common theme in debates about normative marriage. Women's complaints and concerns about marriage are well-known, and those expressed by men are surprisingly similar.

Barbara Ehrenreich (1983) summarizes the important challenges to normative marriage by men in the last half of the twentieth century: "In the 1950s there was a firm expectation that required men to grow up, marry and support their wives. To do anything else was less than grown-up and the man who willfully deviated was judged to be somehow 'less than a man'. By the end of the 1970s and the beginning of the 1980s adult manhood was no longer burdened with the automatic expectation of marriage and breadwinning" (11–12).

Until the 1960s, men's adult lives were defined by marriage. As mature adults they were "good providers." Ehrenreich demonstrates how powerfully convincing the associations among maturity, normality, masculinity, and marriage were in the first half of this century: "If adult masculinity was indistinguishable from the breadwinner role, then it followed that the man who failed to achieve this role was either not fully adult or not fully masculine" (1983: 20). Men who could not, or did not, adequately provide for their wives and families were not only failures, they were not men (they were "pseudo-homosexuals," men who did not meet the prevailing standards of masculinity that were almost entirely related to marriage and the family).

Signs of male rebellion against normative marriage began in the mid-1950s with the image of the "playboy." The image of man portrayed in *Playboy* magazine challenged the prevailing assumption that masculinity was defined by marriage. More specifically, *Playboy* challenged the breadwinning role in marriage as the definition of masculinity:

> When, in the first issue, Hefner talked about staying in his apartment, listening to music and discussing Picasso, there was the Marilyn Monroe centerfold to let you know there was nothing queer about these urbane and indoor pleasures. When the articles railed against the responsibilities of marriage, there were the nude torsos to reassure you that the alternative was still within the bounds of heterosexuality.... In every issue, every month, there was a Playmate to prove that a playboy didn't have to be a husband to be a man. (Ehrenreich, 1983: 51)

It was also during the 1950s that medical opinion expanded the critique of the breadwinner-husband role for men. The "stress" of the hard-driving, unrelentingly ambitious middle-class husband's life was identified as a cause of coronary heart disease, a growing killer of men. The "Type A" personality was the reason for such morbidity and mortality. Men were advised to relax, spend more time sleeping, and assume less responsibility (Friedman and Rosenman, 1974).

The critique of the breadwinning role of husbands was joined by feminists in the late 1960s and early 1970s. Feminism signaled an open questioning of women's traditional dependence on their husbands. The goal of equality between the sexes implied that women would no longer occupy their separate sphere—as home-makers and mothers—nor would women continue to be economically dependent on men. From men's perspectives, this also meant that men would not be expected to be the sole providers for their families—a continuation of the questioning of this role that had begun 20 years earlier. By the 1980s, the critique of the tradi-tional breadwinner/husband role was a central theme of contemporary feminism. More specifically, the association of marriage, breadwinning, and masculinity had been challenged. Traditional definitions of masculinity that defined men by their roles as husbands and providers had been challenged from both sides, by men and women alike.

Sexual Activity

The late 1960s and early 1970s were also known for challenges to traditional sexual norms. However, with the exception of a very few radical critics of marriage, the idea of *fidelity* in marriage was never seriously questioned. For example, the widely discussed *Open Marriage* by Nina and George O'Neill (1972) proposed that mar-ried couples no longer restrict their sexual lives to one another. However, Ameri-can couples who accepted the challenge of "swinging" discovered that it was not likely to bring spouses closer together or promote stability. Indeed, Nina O'Neill recanted seven years later (1977). However, sex in *nonmarital* relationships was a different thing. Premarital sex was certainly much more common in 1970 than it had been 20 years earlier. And it is more common today than a decade ago. Yet marriage has retained its sexually exclusive motif, despite such changes outside the institution. There are now alternatives to marriage for the purpose of sexual rela-tions. It is clear that major changes have occurred in sexual behavior in America. Still, there has been no focused and widespread attempt to modify the sexual as-sumptions of normative marriage. These remain intact despite widespread changes in sexual behaviors among unmarried people.

The attempt to sanction homosexual marriages is certainly a challenge to the heterosexual requirement of normative marriage. And in certain respects, the de-bate about this illustrates the enormously symbolic significance of heterosexuality in normative marriage. In fact, even if homosexuals were allowed to marry, the numbers of such unions would probably be quite small. Although there is no offi-cial count of the number of homosexuals in America, there is emerging consensus from repeated scientific national surveys that only 2%–3% of Americans think of themselves as sexually oriented toward a member of the same sex, even though three times as many report that they have "ever done something sexual with a member of the same sex" (Laumann, Gagnon, Michael, and Michaels, 1994: 294).

The resistance to homosexual marriages, therefore, is based more on normative beliefs than on concern about practical consequences.

Even though there is some evidence that homosexuals are advancing their cause with respect to marriage, the very strong resistance is clear evidence of the enduring and persisting association of marriage and heterosexuality. Even while tolerating homosexuality as a personal orientation, and while accepting homosexuals as colleagues, Americans appear unwilling to redefine marriage to include them.

In reaction to the likely possibility that homosexual marriages will be declared legal in Hawaii, and therefore considered legal in all other states, the U.S. Congress passed an historic "Defense of Marriage Act" in September 1996, allowing states to declare such Hawaiian marriages void in their jurisdictions.

Childbearing

The dramatic increase in nonmarital childbearing since 1960 is a direct challenge to the connection between marriage and childbearing. Is such a trend evidence of widespread rejection of this traditional element of marriage? The social and legal stigmas associated with childbearing outside of marriage have been significantly reduced in many ways in the past two decades. The increase in such births has been accompanied by a corresponding increase in the federal government's support of unmarried mothers and their children. The correlation between these two trends has provoked great debate about whether "generous" welfare payments have *caused* the increase or whether they *result* from such behaviors. If the former, then the "blame" for the increase in nonmarital childbearing must be attributed partially to federal and state social policy that made it possible for men and women to engage in behavior that, heretofore, was less socially acceptable. After an extensive review of the empirical evidence on the subject, Garfinkel and McLanahan (1986) concluded that increases in welfare benefits from 1960 to 1975 led to a small increase (somewhere between 9% and 14%) in the prevalence of single motherhood. The overall increase must be attributed to other factors. Other researchers have come to the same conclusion. Bane and Jargowsky summarize their findings about the role of government policy in industrial societies succinctly: "Direct government policy is neither the problem nor the solution, at least in terms of 'causing' or 'preventing' marital breakup and unmarried parenthood" (1988: 245).

The meaning of increased nonmarital childbearing is found in the cultural understanding and meaning of sexual intercourse. A traditional sociological definition of the institution of marriage interprets it as a way of distributing the obligations that come, inevitably, as a result of coitus. In an earlier time, the connection between sex and pregnancy was taken for granted and informed the cultural meaning of intercourse. Marriage, therefore, has been the socially regulated method of distributing responsibilities for the children produced by intercourse. Parenthood was as integral to the concept of marriage as sexual intercourse because the two were so inherently linked.

Once intercourse and pregnancy were effectively separated by contraceptives, the connection between sex and marriage was also weakened. Effective contraception introduced an historically new question in adult life. Once men and women could limit their fertility, it became possible to ask *why* someone became pregnant. Pregnancy and fertility came to be defined as the result of rational individual choice (despite obvious instances to the contrary). Once parenthood became a choice or decision, it also became a reflection of the individual who decided to bear a child. Parenthood, in short, began to be discussed in terms of individual *motives*. The answers to the question "Why did someone have a child?" are many, but "because he or she is married" is no longer taken for granted.

Since childbearing has come to be seen as a "choice," the role of fathers has curiously changed in at least one way. Childbearing is now perceived as a decision made chiefly by *women*, and the woman who decides to have children is unique. Assumedly, mothers are women who, above all else, will *not* strive for occupational success. Women who accept the premise of innate male-female differences marry earlier and desire, and have, more children than do less traditional women. Traditional women who become mothers are more likely to be housewives and are less likely to have attended college, to have held professional jobs, or to be currently employed (Nock, 1988; Spain and Bianchi, 1996).

Traditional Roles

Part of the feminist critique of traditional marriage in the 1960s and 1970s identified the exclusive homemaker-mother role for women as oppressive. And, of course, such homemakers today are the statistical exception. The Women's Movement was not the cause of the entry of women into paid labor, but it did provide ideological justification and support for what the economy appeared to demand. Only a small minority (28%) of Americans believe that a woman's "place" is in the home, raising children (General Social Surveys, 1994). The combination of economic necessity and changes in assumptions about gender have made motherhood less central as the *sole* adult role of women, married or not.

Maternity must now compete with several other adult roles viewed as important to women today. Childbearing is seen as a *part* of an adult life and identity, and children are significant components of a woman's opportunities in life. Whereas women have traditionally been cast in the role of producers of good children, they are now increasingly consumers—selecting carefully the timing, number, and spacing of births. Childbearing, in short, has become a woman's privilege and right. Women may decide if, when, and how many times they will have children. In this way, childbearing has been redefined as a personal choice. But it is a *woman's* choice more than a man's. The U.S. Supreme Court declared as unconstitutional state laws requiring a husband's consent for his wife's abortion and laws requiring that he be notified before an abortion might be performed (Krause, 1995: 143–44).

Childbearing outside of marriage is certainly more common and acceptable today than in the past, yet this probably says more about contraception than about marriage. Within marriage, childbearing is still virtually ubiquitous. Even though women may have been released from their exclusive roles as mothers and home-makers, there has been little evidence that married couples have rejected the idea of children as a central part of their lives.

The assumption that the husband is the head of the family has been challenged. In the course of two or three decades, husbands have become less central in the lives of wives and families. At the same time, the close association of men's roles in marriage and assumptions about their masculinity has been questioned. More specifically, the idea that to be a man means to be a husband who provides for a wife and family has been repeatedly challenged by diverse groups of men and women. Does this mean that the association no longer remains in our collective minds? Is the definition of masculinity today no longer connected to men's roles as husbands and fathers? Can men be "men" without marrying? Are there alternative ways of being a man?

Before I answer this question, consider the response to the challenges to normative marriage. Is the average American man now less driven to be a married breadwinner? Has he discovered alternative routes to adult male status? Have the gender roles of contemporary marriages become softer and more flexible? Have things really changed for men? Or are they similar to what they were before the "Playboy" philosophy was introduced and the warnings about Type A behavior popularized? The honest answer to all of these questions is "Yes." Things really have changed. And things are pretty much the way they have always been. The normative dimensions of marriage in America have changed in the course of two or three decades. However, the changes, quantitative rather than qualitative, are matters of degree. Our own marriages may differ from our parents', yet they do not differ that much. More particularly, the changes in marriage have focused much more directly on women than on men. Thus, there is still a connection between marriage and masculinity. It is through their marriages, more than any other way, that men conform to shared ideals of manhood. The behaviors and values involved translate into greater success, greater involvement in the community, and greater philanthropy—topics to be discussed later.

Defining Marriage

I refer to the institutionalized aspect of matrimony as normative marriage to reflect the fact that social norms define it. Yet not all such norms are equally compelling. To be a husband means that one is expected to act in predictable ways, but individual men interpret and understand these expectations differently. Such differences, however, fall within a rather narrow range. So, even while men may express themselves differently as husbands, broad similarities among them are the expression of a cultural definition of this role in marriage.

To illustrate this point, consider the normative expectation that spouses are sexually faithful. National surveys have shown repeatedly that Americans view extramarital sex as more reprehensible than most other kinds of sex. When asked about sex before marriage, sex between 14- to 16-year-olds, sex between people of the same sex, and sex with someone other than a spouse, the following percentages of Americans described each type of sex as "Always Wrong" in 1993 (General Social Surveys, 1994):

	Percentage Saying "Always Wrong"
Sex before marriage	27%
Sex between 14- to 16-year-olds	69%
Sex between adults of the same sex	66%
Extramarital sex	77%

These findings suggest widespread agreement about the importance of sexual fidelity in marriage. That is hardly surprising. It would be difficult to imagine any single aspect of marriage more central than sexual exclusivity, and the vast majority of married people do not routinely engage in extramarital affairs. This marriage norm is part of all Western religions. Extramarital sex, moreover, is a crime in some states today and was in all states until recently. Yet, even in the face of social, religious, and legal proscriptions, some married people engage in extramarital sex. Results of a recent national survey show that among those whose marriages are intact, 15% of men and 5% of women admit to having had an extramarital relationship. When those whose marriages are no longer intact are included, these percentages rise only slightly, to 25% for men and 10% for women (Laumann et al., 1994: Table 5.14). And, as the survey results above show, about a quarter of Americans find extramarital sex not "always wrong." As with all social institutions, the rules that govern marriage, either normative or legal, are soft boundaries. They are occasionally crossed by some but never crossed by most. This cannot be said of other types of intimate relationships, however. This institutionalized nature of marriage makes it *qualitatively* different from all other unions of adults.

A normative definition of marriage enumerates the rules accepted as legitimate and binding and explains how and why marriages differ from all other relationships. Since there is no cultural dictionary to provide such a definition, it is necessary to look elsewhere to find the basic rules that govern the institution. Here the task is to identify the core elements that elicit broad consensus. Clues to the meaning of marriage can be found in various measures of public opinion, in law, and in religion.

Public opinion surveys offer insight about the degree of consensus on many issues related to marriage and the family. An overwhelming majority response of Americans to questions about marriage indicates broad consensus on the issues. Of course, what people say in response to survey questions and what people do are sometimes (though not usually) different. When 8 in 10 Americans tell survey researchers that extramarital sex is "always wrong" but only 3 in 10 say the same thing about premarital sex, we have broad consensus on these two issues. Most Americans, that is, think adultery is always wrong. Most think premarital sex is not always wrong.

Domestic relations laws also provide insight about how marriage is defined. Marriage laws are an index of shared ideals and values. State domestic relations laws may be taken as public statements about the way family relations should be. They express the proper, accepted, and moral patterns that are collectively endorsed. In fact, family law addresses issues of personal morality more directly than any other type of law.

Still, family law is only a partial index of all contemporary matrimonial and family values. Because changes in such laws are typically slow, they sometimes reflect values that many question and some reject. For example, half of the U.S. states define sex before marriage (i.e., fornication) as a crime (Krause, 1995: sec. 9.3). Yet the vast majority of young people in America (8 in 10 males and 7 in 10 females under the age of 20) engage in premarital sex (Hayes, 1987), and most Americans say that such behavior is not always wrong. Clearly, laws against fornication are ignored, viewed as an illegitimate area for state intervention. Most young adults view premarital chastity as relatively unimportant. Thus, the idea that unmarried people should refrain from sex is *not* a norm in America, even though it may be the law. Family law is a conservative statement of consensual norms about marriage even though sometimes the law and most Americans' behaviors diverge.

Religion is an even more conservative source of insight into the normative definition of marriage because it changes more slowly than the law. However, the church plays an important role in the way people understand marriage and the family. Americans as a whole are very religious; more than 9 in 10 Americans claim to have a religious affiliation, and involvement in religious activities such as attendance at services is quite high. More than 8 in 10 (83%) Americans attend church, with 35% attending at least weekly. And 6 in 10 Americans pray *at least* daily (General Social Surveys, 1994). Religion also figures importantly in how spouses are selected. Overall, 9 in 10 marriages in this country are between people of the same religious background (General Social Surveys, 1994; Glenn, 1982). The majority of Americans (58%) say that religious beliefs are important in influencing their sexual behaviors (National Health and Social Life Survey, 1992), and 8 in 10 weddings are celebrated in a church or synagogue (Duvall and Miller, 1985).

When public opinion and slowly evolving law or religion appear to be at odds, we may infer the significance of the issue. For example, a public debate about the possibility of legalized homosexual marriages provides clues about how strongly heterosexuality is embedded in the normative definition of American marriage. Such a debate highlights the centrality of issues involved and reveals the magnitude of sentiment associated with them (Hunter, 1991).

I now turn to a consideration of those dimensions of marriage that define the institution.

Individual Free Choice

The most widely shared normative aspect of contemporary marriage is the strong association between it and love. Mate selection in this country has increasingly become a matter of personal choice in which parents play a smaller and smaller role. The contemporary centrality of romantic love for marriage is a fairly recent norm, and historians have documented the gradual evolution of love and the decline of courtship as guiding principles in mate selection (Bailey, 1988; Rothman, 1984). When marriage was the central economic institution, young people inherited their family name and estates. Family alliances were a key function of marriage (especially for women), and love was not seen as a stable basis for such important considerations (Goode, 1970).

The growth of cities, the increase in geographic mobility, and the changing roles of young people fostered a new type of mate selection in the early twentieth century. By the late nineteenth and early twentieth centuries, school attendance was mandatory during the teenage years, a time now known as adolescence. The growing importance of regular and structured education of youths is reflected in employment statistics for the early twentieth century. In 1910, half of all 15-year-old American boys were gainfully employed. By 1930, that proportion was down to only one-sixth. As historian John Modell argues, these pronounced changes reflected a fundamental change in family economies: "The age at which children would begin 'paying back' their parents for the investments they had made in them was postponed over this period for two years or longer, the greater part of this change coming in the 1920s" (1989: 79). Limited more and more to their roles as high school students, young people found new outlets for their free time. Dance halls and movie palaces were popular forms of adolescent recreation in the early twentieth century. "Between 1921 and 1930, average weekly attendance at motion pictures increased rapidly. A weekly movie habit, or more, was typical of unmarried youth, who characteristically attended with age peers" (Modell, 1989: 73). This form of recreation quickly supplanted the older type of mate selection—courtships. Dating, an entirely new form of casual mixed-gender relationship, grew to prominence in the 1920s.

Dating (unlike courtship) stressed attractiveness, thrills, and affection above the more traditional concerns about family name and economic position. But, more important, dating was peer-supervised. A date was something one did *away* from home, unchaperoned by parents. Young people, themselves, made decisions about "getting serious."

The significance of dating centers on whose rules mattered. The rules of courtship—the normative definition of mate selection—traditionally had been the province of parents (especially the girl's parents). The new form of mate selection was also subject to parental influence but was more directly guided by peers. And "success" in the dating process had implications for young people. Dating imposed strong pressures on young people to conform to widely shared standards. A young person's reputation depended largely on success in the dating market, on how he or she "rated" as dates (Nock, 1993: 32).

The children of the dating pioneers of the early 1920s came of age in the early and mid-1950s, by which time dating was firmly established as the dominant and uncontroversial form of mate selection. As James Coleman's (1971) research on high school students in the 1960s revealed, popularity among students was directly tied to peer-established criteria: athletic prowess and attractiveness. Since the 1960s, autonomy in mate selection has continued to increase. Dating is less directly connected to marriage than it once was, and marriages occur later and later in life. However, the central fact in mate selection today is individual choice. Moreover, individual choice is based on questions of compatibility, attractiveness, "value similarity," and other aspects of love.

In fact, most Americans presume that marriage follows "falling in love" and that love is the core element in marriage. In a national study of husbands and wives, "love" was the most frequently cited reason for marrying one's spouse (Pietropinto and Simenauer, 1979). And in an analysis of mate selection in a regional Detroit sample, Martin Whyte found that, when asked which qualities would be most important in making a successful marriage, "respondents say that the emotional, rather than the practical, aspects of marriage are most important in producing success. . . . In picking the single most important trait 'being deeply in love' is ranked after 'satisfying each other's needs'" (1990: 135). Americans marry for love or emotional satisfaction. And the insistence that love is the core of marriage is nowhere better illustrated than in laws governing divorce. In every state, a divorce is permitted when love fails (variously described as "incompatibility" or "irreconcilable differences"). Traditional religious marriage ceremonies admonish spouses to vow to love one another until death.

The close association of love and marriage has important consequences for the way marriage is anticipated, understood, and experienced. Love is associated with feelings of security, comfort, and companionship (Rubin, 1973). The security and presumed stability found in a loving relationship is one reason why the end of such unions is so difficult. Love, most believe, should endure. This belief is held so strongly that a distinction is drawn between "real" love and fleeting love, or infatuation. Ideally, love lasts a lifetime and lovers stay committed forever. Love also implies an erotic component that means lovers experience one another's physical presence as pleasing and stimulating. Romantic love, the hallmark of American courtship (and the greeting card industry), overlooks faults and glorifies and idealizes the other. It supplies emotional gratification when one sacrifices for, or provides for, one's beloved.

To the extent that marriage and love are associated, marriage also implies security, companionship, lifelong commitment, erotic attraction, idealization, and altruism. These characteristics are expected from love and from marriage. Moreover, since mate choice is an individual decision guided by love, the significance and meaning of marriage are quite personal. The external reasons and justifications for marriage that once formed the mate selection process are relatively insignificant. Marriage is a reflection of personal choice, an expression of one's individual personality. Success and failure in marriage are personal successes or failures that cannot easily be attributed to others. This means that mate selection is governed by market principles. Each individual has certain traits that define his or her *value* in the marriage market. So success or failure is related to the possession or development of such traits.

Maturity

For most people, marriage is associated with maturity and adulthood. American laws and customs reflect such assumptions. Because there are few generally recognizable ways of indicating one is mature and normal, marriage becomes important as a sign or validation of maturity.

Domestic relations laws define an age at which individuals may marry. Throughout the United States, the minimum age is usually 18, although marriage is permissible at earlier ages with the court's approval for various reasons. Presumably, such laws protect youths from the premature assumption of adult responsibilities (O'Donnell and Jones, 1982: 36). Historically, the minimum age requirements for marriage in common law were designed to correspond with sexual and procreational abilities and were consistent with the actual assumptions of adult responsibilities, the ages at which people began having children, and the length of life (Wadlington and Paulsen, 1978). Today, such laws reflect the presumption that these adults can enter into a contract.

The minimum age at marriage is also the age at which youths are legally emancipated. Parental responsibility for care and support is terminated upon emancipation. Thus, the minimum marriage age and the legal emancipation age are the same. Marriage, in short, may occur when parents are released from their legal obligations to their children—that is, when children are presumed to be mature and capable of self-sufficiency.

In the traditional Judeo-Christian wedding ceremony, each newly married partner is described as free from the parental home and dependence upon it. A new form of maturity quite different from the dependency of a child is celebrated.

"A man leaves his father and mother and cleaves to his wife and they become one flesh" (Genesis 2: 24).

Maturity and independence are closely related concepts, and most Americans associate independence with marriage. Living arrangements illustrate this point clearly. Newly married couples in America typically establish a new residence, often miles from either set of parents. Only 3% of married persons live with a parent (U.S. Bureau of the Census, 1994: Table 1). Very few married couples receive significant routine financial assistance from parents, and parental assistance declines as children age, dropping off rather quickly in young adulthood. By age 45, fewer than one in five married adults with living parents receives regular assistance of any sort (child care, advice, gifts, income, time; Cooney and Uhlenberg, 1992). Although parents give their adult children substantial time and money when the children are establishing households and families, and when the parents themselves are middle-aged, most assistance is in the form of time, babysitting, and other services. In fact, the average annual amount of money transferred from parent to child in the late 1980s ranged from $1,500 to $2,000 (Soldo and Hill, 1993: 200–1).

Heterosexuality

For most of history, the only acceptable form of sex was with one's spouse. Even sex within marriage has been restricted to conventional forms of expression. Spouses legally are not permitted to engage in certain forms of sexual behaviors. Generally, anything other than marital vaginal intercourse has been prohibited by law. Legal scholars O'Donnell and Jones note that sodomy laws that define other types of sex as criminal are expressions of the "genital-use" hierarchy that refers to how genitals are used in sexual expression. When genitals are used in any way that departs from their symbolic significance as implements of reproduction, these acts may be viewed as "profanations" and will be ranked accordingly. The more the sexual act departs from heterosexual vaginal intercourse, in other words, the greater is the offense and the more "objectified" the use of the genital:

> Historically, stratified profanations have ranged from nonreproductive intercourse, through such methods of noncoital expression as mutual masturbation, artificially assisted organism, oral copulation, and anal copulation, to various methods of interaction that involve the possibility of injury or pain. Legal responses to these stratified uses, in turn, have ranged from the now-unconstitutional restraints on contraception to battery laws. Generally the severity of these penalties has paralleled the extent to which genital use has been objectified. (1982: 24–25)

Laws have addressed same-sex unions, and despite concerted efforts to legalize them, people of the same sex are forbidden to marry. And even though there is growing acceptance of homosexuality in general, public support for homosexual marriage has not followed. As a practical matter, homosexuality, because it is a crime in many jurisdictions, would seem to preclude legal same-sex marriages. Even if homosexuality were to be decriminalized, there is no necessary reason that homosexual marriages would be legalized (Krause, 1995: 46). Recent attempts to sanction homosexual unions as marriages have been strongly resisted. The resistance is best seen as a struggle to redefine normative marriage. Indeed, sociologist James Hunter claims that homosexuality is a key issue over which Americans find themselves clearly divided and competing to define the norms of American life. He believes that with the possible exception of abortion, "few issues in the contemporary culture war generate more raw emotion than the issue of homosexuality [because] few other issues challenge the traditional assumptions of what nature will allow, the boundaries of the moral order, and finally the ideals of middle-class family life more radically" (1989: 189). As Hunter notes, proposals to legalize homosexual marriages are a challenge to the traditional conception of marriage. And that is the central point. Heterosexuality is part of the traditional conception of marriage.

Husband As Head

Marriage has traditionally defined husbands as the head of the family. Married women have assumed their husband's social and legal identities, as well as their surnames. At the same time, it is fair to say that Americans generally favor equality between the sexes. But wives and husbands occupy different positions in marriage.

The traditional assumption that men would be the primary breadwinners and wives would be the primary homemakers/child-rearers has been replaced by an assumption that men and women should share such tasks. Indeed, the majority of married women today work outside the home, as do two-thirds (68%) of wives with young children (Spain and Bianchi, 1996).

The General Social Surveys show the extent to which Americans believe in task sharing in these areas of marriage (questions asked in between 1988 and 1991; sample size 2,725).

	Percentage Who Agree
1. All in all, family life suffers when the woman has a full-time job.	34%
2. Both the husband and wife should contribute to the household income	48%
3. A husband's job is to earn money; a wife's job is to look after the home and family	28%
4. It is much better for everyone involved if the man is the achiever outside the home and the woman takes care of the home and family	40%

Although there is a general tendency toward less traditional marital roles, little consensus exists. The majority of Americans hold some egalitarian views about spouses (i.e., only a third believe that family life suffers when the wife works; only a quarter believe that the wife's job is to look after the home). However, only half believe that both spouses should contribute to family income. And 4 in 10 Americans endorse a very traditional division of roles, with the wife taking care of the home and family and the husband earning the income. Such sentiments are reflected in actual behaviors.

In fact, husbands typically *do* have earnings much greater than their wives, and the responsibility for homemaking and child care actually *does* fall disproportionately on wives today as it has for decades. Working wives contribute about 30% of their family's income. The percentage is only slightly higher (40%) in those families in which the wife worked full-time, year-round. The presence of children, especially preschoolers, reduces the likelihood that a wife works, as well as the amount she earns if she does work (Bianchi, 1995: 143). Married mothers do about two-thirds of all housework. Although this is a decline over what they did a decade earlier, it is not large enough to compensate for the increase in paid labor-force time for which wives are now responsible (Robinson, 1988).

Even in the most "egalitarian" of marriages, an extensive division of tasks emerges over time and allocates husbands' and wives' responsibilities. Our cultural understanding of the relative position of men and women in marriage derives from these details. Household tasks are quite strongly related to gender. Husbands participate most in yard/home maintenance and child care; they also do about 40 percent of the family workload in these two areas (Goldscheider and Waite, 1991: ch. 7). Husbands do less than a quarter of cooking, housecleaning, dish washing, and laundry chores.

The arrival of a child typically leads to greater "traditionalization" in the arrangement of household tasks. Sociologists Ralph and Maureen LaRossa (1981) found that the arrival of a new baby often results in mothers becoming the primary care givers and fathers becoming the primary wage earners, regardless of how things were done before the child was born. Most researchers attribute this common pattern to rational allocation of labor by couples. "If and when the question arose as to who should cut back on labor-force participation to accommodate the needs of children, the women curtailed their labor-force participation more so than did their husbands. During the 1980s, women—even well-educated women—continued to have difficulty sustaining their earnings position relative to men across the life cycle" (Bianchi, 1995: 435).

We have yet to identify all the causes of differential involvement in paid labor or housework. Regardless of the reasons, however, this pattern is evident in contemporary marriages. But whether the pervasive division of tasks amounts to differential power and authority is another question. It is safe to conclude, however, that most researchers, as well as most married couples, attribute greater importance to family income than to most other parts of family life. Beside income, most other aspects of household maintenance are secondary. The spouse who is primarily responsible for this crucial asset, therefore, typically enjoys greater authority. And, because the husband customarily has the greater earnings potential, his position in the family is enhanced. The demands of his job have priority over most other family concerns. He is able to translate his responsibilities at work into demands on the family. Because such demands are understandable and may appear legitimate, they are accorded greater legitimacy than others. Thus, in most American marriages husbands have greater authority than their wives, regardless of professed ideology.

Fidelity and Monogamy

Traditionally, marriage was the only acceptable venue for sex. Though commonplace today, sex before marriage is still defined as a crime (fornication) in half of all U.S. states (Krause, 1995: sec. 9.9). In law, sex is the symbolic core of marriage, defining it in more obvious and restrictive ways than any other. To understand the symbolic significance of sex, one can analyze sex in marriage as a form of *property.*

Property is not a thing, per se, but a social relationship among individuals who agree how to behave toward a particular thing. To own something does not imply a bond to that particular item. Instead, it means that (1) you have a right to use it, (2) other people do not have the right to use it, and (3) you can call on the rest of society to enforce your rights (Collins and Coltrane, 1991: 53). Sex in marriage satisfies these three conditions: husbands and wives have a right to have sexual intercourse with one another, other people do not have a right to sexual intercourse with either of them while they are married, and either spouse can enlist the assistance of society to enforce his or her sexual rights (e.g., divorce or adultery charges). As a form of marital property, nothing is so important, nor governed by more rules, than sex.

In common law, a marriage was protected from damage that might be done to it, either intentionally or accidentally, by spouses or outside parties. Historically, the law has recognized the vulnerability and potential fragility of the marital relationship and protected this interest through the concept of *consortium.* "Such elements as domestic duties, interaction, affectional intimacy, love, and sexual intercourse are among the factors typically recognized under the law, and when their infringement is deemed an offense according to statute or court decision, monetary damages can be exacted" (O'Donnell and Jones, 1982: 66). Traditionally, only the husband was entitled to sue for injuries relating to his wife. In addition to recovery for injury to the wife herself, the husband would be compensated for damage to his relational interest in his wife. According to Krause, "Today, loss of consortium actually has gained in importance as a factor in tort actions, because a majority of recent cases has concluded that the wife has an equivalent right to recover for loss of her husband's consortium" (1995: 138).

Damage done to a marriage by one of the spouses has typically been handled by divorce law. Accidental or intentional damages to a marriage by third parties, however, have been handled as consortium offenses. Negligent damage to consortium is illustrated by the case of a serious injury to a spouse that makes that person unable to have sexual intercourse. In such a case, the flow of consortium is reduced and the negligent party may be liable for damages. Intentional damage to consortium includes three torts for which monetary damages may be awarded: enticement, alienation of affections, and criminal conversation.

In the case of enticement, a third party intentionally and knowingly causes one spouse to separate or remain separated from the other without the latter's consent, for illegitimate reasons (marital disruption, for example; O'Donnell and Jones, 1982: 70). A lover's affections and attentions may cause a spouse to leave his or her marriage. Alienation of affections occurs when the emotional attraction between spouses is broken by the intentional efforts of others. Parents or friends may intentionally attempt to convince one spouse to leave the other, for example. Such cases have been the grounds for lawsuits and the award of monetary damages.

The most serious damage to consortium, however, is criminal conversation, otherwise known as adultery. Because sexual exclusivity is the core of marriage, this type of offense may threaten the marriage itself. Indeed, adultery is so serious a threat to marriage that the homicides sometimes provoked by the discovery of it may be treated differently than other forms, reducing murder to manslaughter: "Even where all elements of voluntary manslaughter are proved in such circumstances, many juries refuse to convict a cuckolded husband" (Krause, 1995: 152). Moreover, the offending third party has traditionally been left virtually without defense. He or she may have been unaware of the existence of a marriage or may have been seduced by the married person. Regardless, the only comprehensive defense was evidence that the suing spouse facilitated the event (consenting to it, or arranging it; O'Donnell and Jones, 1982: 72).

Closely related to fidelity is monogamy. Almost all states have vigorously enforced laws that forbid any type of multiple marriage. However, it is not entirely clear why. In 1878, the U.S. Supreme Court upheld the conviction of a Mormon who had practiced polygamy in accordance with his religious beliefs. The justification used by the Court in *Reynolds* was that the First Amendment prohibits the use of laws to restrict religious beliefs, but not religious practices. This argument made sense because certainly some actions might be called for by religion that would be dangerous or disruptive (e.g., ritual human sacrifice). The Court also justified its decision by noting that polygamy, although widely practiced throughout the world, has never been acceptable in the West. Further, the Court noted, monogamy is consistent with democracy, whereas polygamy lent itself to despotism. Some have questioned whether these justifications are sufficient, today, to overcome the fundamental right that all Americans now enjoy to marry (O'Donnell and Jones, 1982: 44). With the exception of the state of Utah, where polygamy is still practiced by some Mormons, this basic aspect of American normative marriage has gone largely unchallenged. And even in Utah, where polygamy is tolerated, it is still illegal (i.e., the law is not enforced).

Monogamy has traditionally implied that one person marry one spouse for life. In light of the very high divorce rate in the United States, however, this is less often the case. About half of marriages end in divorce or are predicted to (McLanahan and Casper, 1995). This high divorce rate should not be interpreted as a rejection of monogamy, but as the adaptation now called "serial monogamy." Most marriages are monogamous for their duration in practice (Laumann et al., 1995). This means that both spouses have agreed, by virtue of the marriage, to restrict themselves from entering the marriage market so long as they are married. No spouse, therefore, may *legitimately* pursue another person for romantic purposes while married. And that is the critical meaning of monogamy.

Parenthood

Few aspects of American life are so constant as the relationship between marriage and parenthood. With very few exceptions, married women and men become mothers and fathers. Indeed, the connection between parenthood and marriage has been so close that the question of whether a married couple would have children is rarely asked. Rather, the question is *when* a married couple will begin having children. Only 1 in 10 (11%) ever-married women are still childless by age 44. And half of all married women younger than 35 who were childless in 1990 reported that they expected to have a child at some point in the future (O'Connell, 1991).

The close association of marriage and childbearing is the reason for the current concern over illegitimacy. The apparent weakening of the link between marriage and childbearing has been the subject of much legal, social, and religious animation for at least two or three decades. The issue of nonmarital childbearing helps us understand the traditional assumptions about parenthood embodied in normative marriage.

When the family was the primary source of social and legal status, sharp distinctions were drawn between children born to married couples and those born outside marriage. The offspring of an unmarried couple was viewed by the Christian church as "sin turned into flesh," because premarital sex is, itself, a sin (Krause, 1995: 164). And in law, children born outside of a legal marriage (i.e., the result of adulterous, bigamous, or incestuous unions, or those born to unmarried women) were denied full legal status and citizenship. Any such child was "illegitimate" and was denied legal inheritance and support prerogatives.

While biology settles questions about who the mother of a child is, social, religious, and legal rules have served to connect every child to an adult male. The simplest such rule, common in this country for over 200 years, is the legal presumption that any child born to a married woman is the offspring of the husband and, ipso facto, the legal child of *both* husband and wife unless there is compelling evidence of the husband's inability to sire a child (O'Donnell and Jones, 1982: 97). Anthropologist Bronislaw Malinowski described this, and other such practices found universally, as the "principle of legitimacy" (Malinowski, 1964). The bastard child traditionally lacked a male link to the larger society/community. The child did not inherit a family name, was not the legal responsibility of any male, and was not seen as part of any known kinship lineage.

Practically, this means that the married parents of any child born during the marriage (or born shortly after marriage) are entitled to custody of that child. Thus, the only action that a man must take to receive custody of a child is to be married to the mother when that child is born (or shortly thereafter). So, while childbirth clearly resolves the maternity question, marriage is the simplest method to establish the more complex issue of paternity. In this sense, marriage is the most elementary method of connecting every child with an adult male who becomes socially responsible for him or her.

The dependency of children is a problem in all societies. By one means or another, the obligations for support and care of children must be distributed. And because mothers have not been able to provide sufficient support alone, marriage has traditionally served this distributional objective. Parental obligations are now based more on blood than marriage. And fathers who are not married may be required to provide for their children through various legal and social mechanisms. However, the married man becomes the social father of children born to his wife with no state involvement. The obligations associated with custody are pervasive and, until recently, gendered. Men have been responsible for providing for their children, just as they have been for supporting their wives. Women, on the other hand, have been responsible for the care and nurture of children.

Custody and parental responsibilities may be viewed as reciprocal concepts. Parental custody conveys both privileges and responsibilities for the care and provision of children. Historically, American parents have been held legally responsible for a child's financial support, health, and education and also for the inculcation of basic attitudes (respect for people and authority). These obligations of parents are balanced by their legal custody of children. Custody entitles parents to discipline, demand services (including wages and salaries), and make all decisions relating to their children's welfare as they see fit. This relationship between parent and child is enforced by law until emancipation (i.e., until the child reaches the age of majority or is, otherwise, legally emancipated).

The primary concern in matters of children and childbearing today is the well-being of the child. Therefore, the numerous legal disabilities suffered by illegitimate children (e.g., limits on inheritance or eligibility for government transfer payments) were declared unconstitutional by the Supreme Court in a number of decisions between 1968 and 1978. A 1972 decision by the Court declares "imposing disabilities on the illegitimate child is contrary to the basic concept of our system that legal burdens should bear some relationship to individual responsibility or wrongdoing. Obviously, no child is responsible for his birth and penalizing the illegitimate child is an ineffectual—as well as unjust—way of deterring the parent" (*Weber v. Aetna Casualty and Surety*, 1972). This and similar decisions were based on the *equal protection* clause of the Fourteenth Amendment.

Parental authority has also been eroded by other legal developments. Children are increasingly viewed in law as independent persons. For certain purposes, parents may not legally interfere with their children's interests. This is most obvious in matters of medical care. When parents assert their parental authority in denying "necessary emergency" medical care (on religious grounds, for example), courts may intervene against the will of the parents and order (through a guardian for the child) that the treatment be provided. In many states, minors may procure an abortion without parental notice or consent, although the U.S. Supreme Court has upheld the legality of laws requiring either (Krause, 1995: ch. 14). Still, parents have enormous authority in matters concerning their children. Parents have even been allowed to assert their religious beliefs in order to remove their children from "mandatory" public schools (*Wisconsin v. Yoder*, 1972).

What difference does it make whether a parent is married? Unmarried fathers, after all, may be legally ordered to support their children. In reality, such support orders are difficult to enforce if fathers do not live with their children. From the child's perspective, having a father who is not married to his or her mother has enormous consequences *if* the man is absent from the home. Such children suffer a wide range of long-term consequences, including lower educational attainments, higher dropout rates, higher teenage pregnancy rates, and higher unemployment rates. The reason for such troubling and firmly established patterns is a matter of debate. Yet there is persuasive evidence that children who live with only one parent (regardless of the reason) lack the pervasive connections to friends, neighbors, parents of peers, and other adults and community institutions that children in two-parent homes enjoy. In short, they lack social capital (Coleman, 1988; McLanahan and Sandefur, 1994).

What about the parent's perspective? Does marriage make a difference? This is the more relevant perspective to consider. In reality, married and unmarried fathers do not enjoy comparable custody rights and associated obligations. It is important to be clear about what is being comparing here. Unmarried fathers may, through various legal petitions, obtain the custody of their children. If they do this, then there is little to distinguish the married and unmarried father. If they do not, however, there are enormous differences. Custody is the most enduring of adult obligations. Parental responsibilities, once assumed, may not be easily abandoned, as divorce proceedings make plain. Although one may have an ex-spouse, there is no ex-child. But unmarried fathers often do not wish to assume the legal or social responsibility for their children. Indeed, a vast arrangement of state and federal mechanisms exists to enforce the parental obligations of men who do not voluntarily assume them. Limitations on the receipt of welfare payments to women who do not cooperate in identifying and locating absent fathers are federal law. Every state must maintain a parent locator service, and these agencies have access to Social Security, Internal Revenue, and other federal databases. The parent locator services are also made available to women who are *not* receiving welfare payments. In 1993, 4.5 million absent parents were located and paternity was established in 550,000 cases, resulting in new support orders in more than a million such instances (Krause, 1995: 265–66). As McLanahan and Sandefur note, paternity establishment rates for children born outside of marriage range from a low of 5.5% in Arizona to a high of 67% in Georgia (1994: 148).

Unmarried men who do not live with the mothers of their children, it would seem, are uninterested in assuming the social and legal role of father to their children. This may also be true of married men. However, married men have enduring and enforceable obligations as fathers. A married man has, by virtue of his status as a husband, *voluntarily* assumed the various responsibilities associated with parenthood. He has, moreover, announced his willingness to do this by marrying his wife. His role as social father to his children is proclaimed by marriage. By his marriage, a man has made a *public* statement about himself as a father, or potential father, and all that goes with this role. Even if his marriage should fail, his parental obligations will not be eliminated, although they may be attenuated. Therefore, marital paternity differs from the nonmarital variety primarily in the public statement it makes about the man.

Gender in Marriage

The model of normative marriage shows the centrality of gender to traditional definitions of the institution. And it is this aspect of marriage that has been criticized most forcefully. Before concluding that modern marriages are still organized by gender, I want to consider how recent events have altered this core aspect of them.

Significant and important changes have occurred in the law. Whereas vestiges of discriminatory laws based on gender in marriage remain, the U.S. Supreme Court has recently ruled on a number of critical cases that have eliminated most such statutes on *equal protection* and *due process* clause bases. Indeed, for most purposes, legal rights and responsibilities in marriage today pertain to "spouses" rather than to "husbands" or "wives."

For example, laws about minimum ages for marriage traditionally specified younger ages for women than men because of the husband's legal obligation to provide for his wife and children. Since the mid-1970s, however, such discrimination has been outlawed. In two *Stanton* cases (1975), the Court ruled that a Utah law requiring parents to support boys until they were 21 but girls only until 18 was unconstitutional. Likewise, the husband's traditional support obligations were much greater than those imposed on the wife. In *Orr v. Orr* (1979) the U.S. Supreme Court imposed equality in matters of alimony (ruling it unconstitutional to require husbands, but not wives, to pay alimony), thereby appearing to mandate equality in matters of support as well (Krause, 1995: 160).

Wives traditionally have assumed their husband's surnames, and those who did not have experienced difficulties in obtaining driver's licenses or registering to vote (Weitzman, 1981). Likewise, the husband's domicile has traditionally been taken to define the married couple's domicile (i.e., a wife was defined as a resident of the state in which the husband lived, and the husband could decide where the couple would live). In *Kirchberg v. Feenstra* (1981) the U.S. Supreme Court invalidated a Louisiana law that gave the husband control of community property. Thus, the husband's role in defining domicile is also, presumably, abrogated.

Although the husband traditionally has enjoyed the right to sue others for causing a loss of consortium with his wife, she seldom had the same options. This is no longer the case. "All but universally today, equivalent rights are extended to the wife or denied to the husband" (Krause, 1995: 161).

As noted earlier, with respect to their marriages, men and women are increasingly viewed as "spouses" rather than "husbands" or "wives." For example, the marital unit has been defined as an entity greater than either partner in it. Spouses are subordinate, in certain respects, to the unity created by their marriage. By virtue of their intimate, ongoing relationship, interdependencies develop that unite the spouses in complex and pervasive ways. Historically, the unity of marriage was "achieved" by abolishing the identity of the wife, who lost autonomy in such things as contracts, credit, earnings, and property (O'Donnell and Jones, 1982: 62). The unity of the marriage has meant that spouses enjoy certain privileges not granted to unmarried persons. For example, husbands and wives have traditionally been able to refuse to testify against one another. And as noted, the law has recognized the interests of spouses in the unity created by their marriage in consortium rights.

In addition to viewing marriage as a unity, the law has also sought to protect the harmony of the relationship. This means that spouses are denied access to the courts in matters pertaining to their own ongoing relationships—wives could not sue husbands, children could not sue parents. Marital harmony, traditionally, is jeopardized by taking intimate disputes to a third party such as a court. Therefore, spouses have been enjoined from suing one another for torts such as negligence (intraspousal tort immunity). And husbands have been immune from prosecution for the rape of their wives. The justification for such intraspousal limitations and immunities is that the involvement of the court in marital disputes is likely to exacerbate them.

In civil suits, the legal trend is to eliminate intraspousal tort immunities altogether because they deny married persons the same protection that unmarried people enjoy. Indeed, the majority of states have eliminated such immunities (Krause, 1995: 137). Similar trends are evident with respect to certain criminal acts. For example, spouse battering has now been defined as a felony in many states (especially when the wife is the victim). Until the 1970s, the husband who raped his wife typically was prosecuted on other grounds, if he was prosecuted at all. The use of force, for example, might bring charges of assault and battery. However, since the mid-to-late 1970s, most states have amended their rape statutes to permit husbands to be charged under certain circumstances. Typically, the husband and wife must be living separately (usually judicial separation) and force must be used for a nonconsensual sexual act to qualify as rape.

The testimonial privilege that spouses have traditionally enjoyed has meant that, for many issues, a spouse might refuse to testify against a partner. This has not been an absolute immunity, because spouses have been allowed to testify about injuries inflicted by the other on that spouse or a child. And when one partner voluntarily offered to testify against another, the issue has sometimes been answered by deciding whose privilege it is, the defendant's or that of the potential witness (Krause, 1995: 151). However, such privileges have now been severely limited or abolished completely. Finally, laws against adultery by married spouses have been abolished in most states, and where such laws exist, they are typically ignored.

In general, states have amended their family laws to reflect a more gender-neutral view of the marriage relationship. This has often meant that the marriage is less significant as an entity and the individuals in it more so. The model of patriarchal marriage is no longer the guide for family law. Increasingly, married persons are treated very much like their unmarried counterparts in law. However, the revisions of family law have concentrated on this one dimension of marriage—the gendered nature of rights and responsibilities. Other dimensions of normative marriage have been largely untouched, including assumptions about individual choice, maturity, heterosexuality, or monogamy. Now that men and women enjoy greater equality outside their families, the law of marriage and marital relationships appears to be catching up.

Lest one conclude that most American marriages are, in fact, very different things today than they were two or three decades ago, one must realize that social change occurs slowly. It may be easier to amend laws than beliefs and easier to change judicial practice than individual behavior. Moreover, the creation and enforcement of laws are sometimes separate issues. In reality, an examination of actual behaviors reveals just how slowly things do change.

Gender equality in a marriage can be evaluated in several ways. Perhaps the best way to begin is by considering how men and women define their marriages. Who do they name as the head of the family? Who makes decisions? The mundane aspects of daily life also provide a clue about the equality between spouses. Who does what and how often? The relative economic positions of spouses may also be considered. When such issues are examined, it becomes clear that marriage is a stable institution that is slow to change.

The U.S. Census Bureau conducts national surveys of approximately 60,000 households each month for purposes of estimating employment, economic, and demographic changes. Until 1980, these surveys defined the husband as the "head of household" or "head of family." Since 1980, however, the questions have used the term "householder" and "family householder." When a married person is interviewed, that person is asked to identify the person in whose name the house or apartment is owned or rented. If there is no such person, any adult member other than roomers, boarders, or employees may be listed. If the house is owned or rented jointly by a married couple, the householder may be either the husband or the wife. What can be inferred by how people answer this question? For one, it gives some indication of who owns married couples' property. Additionally, when property is jointly owned (as real estate commonly is in marriage), responses offer some insight into which spouse is most commonly mentioned as the "reference" person. There is no particular reason to believe that either partner would be listed more frequently in such cases. Therefore, to the extent that one or the other does dominate, something is revealed about how marriages are described by married people.

In 1994, 91% of married individuals living with a spouse named the husband as the householder (personal communication with Arlene Saluter, U.S. Bureau of the Census, October 25, 1995). In 1980, this figure was 96% (Smith, 1992). It would appear that a growing number of American couples define the wife as the head of the household. Nonetheless, the extremely high percentage of married individuals (both male and female) who describe the householder as the husband surely offers little evidence of major restructuring of the male-as-head-of-household practice.

The allocation of time and effort in the home is a reflection of economic concerns (whose time is most economically valuable; Becker, 1981), tradition, ideas about fairness and equity, and differential power (England and Farkas, 1986; Huber and Spitze, 1983). Whatever the reason for the particular division of tasks in a married household, the complex arrangement results from many small and large decisions and tells us a great deal about how the relationship is organized.

The allocation of tasks within the household is strongly related to participation in the paid labor force. Married women have entered the labor force in increasing numbers for four decades with corresponding shifts in household labor. In 1960, a third (32%) of married women were in the labor force. In 1993, almost 6 in 10 (59%) were (Spain and Bianchi, 1996). Wives now work fewer hours than their husbands, but the difference is declining. In 1975, married women worked an average of 30.2 hours per week compared with 45.8 for married men. This 15-hour difference had dropped to 11 hours by 1987 (48.3 for married men, 37.4 for married women). However, unmarried men and women have more similar work-ing hours today than married couples and have since at least 1975 (Shelton, 1992). Marriage, it seems, is associated with *greater* differences between men and women in the hours committed to paid labor.

It is not surprising to discover, therefore, that among employed husbands and wives, housework is still primarily the wife's work. In 1975, women did about 2.5 times as much housework as their husbands did (10.7 hours per week for hus-bands and 25.3 hours per week for wives). By 1981, the ratio was down to 2.1 and had dropped to 1.9 by 1987. Even though it is tempting to conclude that the grad-ual shift over time reflects the increasing hours women are spending at paid work, multivariate analysis that includes time in the labor force and marital status (as well as children and age) reveals that married women spend over five more hours per week on household labor than single women, whereas married men spend two fewer hours on household labor than single men (Shelton, 1992: Table 4.13). In other words, even after consideration of the increasing amount of time spent at work, married women still do more household labor than their husbands and do more than unmarried women. The changes over time have as much to do with the fact that married women are spending fewer hours maintaining homes and chil-dren today than they were years ago as they do with actual shifts in relative re-sponsibilities. And much of the difference between husbands' and wives' home-making time can be attributed to differential involvements in the care of children. When preschool-age children are present in the household, wives' housework in-creases, yet husbands' remains essentially unchanged. "Getting married and hav-ing children affect women's household labor time far more than they affect men's. . . . The increase in women's labor-force participation as well as the increase in their paid labor time is not accompanied by a commensurate decrease in women's household labor time" (Shelton, 1992: 108).

How are such findings to be interpreted? On the one hand, there is some evi-dence of minor changes in the division of tasks and responsibilities among married couples. But only a little. Women have increased their involvement in paid labor, but their husbands have taken up little of the slack in homemaking. After examin-ing the meaning of these issues to married couples, sociologist Arlie Hochschild found that they are a major source of tension and perceived inequity. Hochschild's intensive research on "the second shift" convinced her that for many couples (per-haps 4 in 10) there is a mismatch between spouses' beliefs about appropriate activ-ities. Typically, wives have come to expect more equality than their mothers expe-rienced in their marriages, but husbands, despite lip service to sharing housework, are less likely to act accordingly (Hochschild and Machung, 1989).

Perhaps such male prerogatives are rational since husbands typically earn more than their wives, despite changes in employment and hours worked (Becker, 1981; see Brines, 1993, for a discussion). Among wives who work, higher-earning wives are married to higher-earning husbands (Levy, 1987). Therefore, the relative earnings of spouses are comparably constant across the range of family incomes. The following figures are computed for married women under age 60 with earnings last year, married to husbands with earnings last year, and living in households with no other adult earners. In such households, household income is, essentially, the sum of the husband's and wife's incomes. Such wives' incomes were 35% of real (1986) household income in the five-year period 1975–1980. The percentage increased to 38% in the period from 1982 to 1985 and was unchanged (37%) for 1986 to 1991 (General Social Surveys, 1994).

If husbands and wives *are* economically rational, one might expect that wives would perform more housework if they are economically dependent on their husbands. And even if the mechanism involves more than pure economic rationality, husbands may still "exchange" income for household labor. In general, wives do more housework and earn less than their husbands. Moreover, wives' housework time appears to vary with the degree of economic dependency on their husbands. However, more than economic exchange drives this process. One researcher (Brines, 1994) showed that a husband's dependency on his wife does *not* translate into greater shares of housework. In fact, husbands who have been unemployed for several months actually *reduce* their housework efforts.

Why would economically dependent husbands do *less* housework and economically dependent wives do *more*? The answer is that housework and the time required to do it are more than simple economic commodities. The details of routine household life, as well as the dependencies associated with them, carry enormous symbolic meaning. "Men's" work means providing for the family and being the "breadwinner," whereas "women's" work means caring for the home and children. These associations are part of the culture and embedded in institutions. They are widely believed by American men and women and are reinforced by economic, religious, and educational institutional arrangements. In short, these associations are more than personal beliefs; they are normative. Doing housework, earning a living, providing for the family, and caring for children are ways of demonstrating masculinity and femininity. When wives are economically dependent on their husbands, doing housework is consistent with the gender assumptions embodied in normative marriage. In such circumstances, women do not deviate from cultural expectations. However, a dependent husband departs from traditional assumptions about marriage. Were he to respond by doing more housework, he would deviate even more. When he does even *less* housework, therefore, he is compensating for his departure from normative assumptions by being more traditional in whatever ways he can.

The presentation of oneself as masculine or feminine is a task of everyday life, one that requires demonstrating appropriate behavior. This is what sociologists West and Zimmerman (1987) called the "doing of gender" and Erving Goffman (1979) called "gender display." As Goffman noted: "If gender is defined as the culturally established correlates of sex (whether in consequence of biology or learning), then gender display refers to conventionalized portrayals of these correlates" (1979: 1). People "know" how to appear, or present themselves, as masculine or feminine because there are cultural stereotypes of these images. Gender stereotypes are applied from an early age, thereby providing each person with a repertoire of acceptable forms of presentations. However, the existence and application of such stereotypes do more than simply provide clues about how to behave among others. In learning how to express oneself, a person is also learning to be masculine or feminine.

Gender displays are not essentially superficial. They are not, in other words, simply one of many ways a person might present himself or herself, much as one might decide to wear a white rather than a striped shirt. They are much more than that. The gender stereotypes from which gender displays are drawn, and from which they derive meanings, are integrated into the fabric of a culture. All social institutions embody them. For that reason, such displays are integrated into the economy, religion, and other basic social structures. This gives gender displays a coercive quality. People who deviate in obvious ways from the customary and ordinary may be treated differently. The effeminate man or the masculine woman may pay prices for their departures from custom and convention, ranging from others' disapproval to objective punishments and losses. There is, in short, an expectation that males present themselves as masculine, and females as feminine. As Goffman says, "Femininity and masculinity are in a sense the prototypes of essential expression—something that can be conveyed fleetingly in any social situation, and yet sommething that strikes at the most basic characterization of the individual" (1979: 7).

The traditional assumptions about gender in marriage are part of the personal identities of husbands and wives. The model of men and women embodied in the cultural ideal of marriage influences how spouses see themselves and how they wish to be seen by others. The title of a book on the division of household labor proclaimed that the family is *The Gender Factory* (Berk, 1985). As the author concluded, "At least metaphorically, the division of household labor facilitates two production processes: the production of goods and services and what we might call the production of gender. Simultaneously, household members 'do' gender, as they 'do' housework and child care. . . . The division of household labor is the mechanism by which both the material and the symbolic products of the household are realized" (Berk, 1985: 201).

Conclusion

Normative marriage is the institution of expectations, laws, beliefs, customs, and assumptions that are part of every marital relationship. Such soft boundaries form part of a husband's and wife's personal identities. Although the same can be said about all social institutions (i.e., normative assumptions influence behaviors and beliefs), there is something special about marriage because of its intimacy and immediacy. It is in the intimacy of married life that men and women define themselves as persons rather than employees, students, voters, faithful believers, or any number of other public identities. One of the most important dimensions of personal identity is gender. It is in families that husbands and wives render themselves accountably masculine and feminine, even though gender, unlike all other social roles, is presumed to transcend virtually all situations (an assumption that will be challenged later).

In this chapter I developed a normative definition of marriage by consulting public opinion, law, and religion. That definition consists of six ideals that constitute the core of the American institution of marriage. Marriage thus defined is a structure, or model, that continually influences and shapes husbands and wives in predictable ways. Most important, marriage contributes to one's sense of being masculine or feminine. For men, especially, masculinity inheres in normative marriage. When attention turns to the role of marriage in defining gender, we will see how the institution influences men in many beneficial ways. That is the goal of the following chapter.

3

Marriage and Masculinity

The next step in connecting marriage and masculinity is to develop a normative definition of masculinity. Like marriage, gender involves a complex system of expectations and rules. Just as one can describe "right" and "wrong" ways of behaving as a husband or wife, so can one describe acting appropriately—or normatively—as a man or a woman.

Theories about gender (specifically, about masculinity) from several social sciences are useful in developing a definition of masculinity. It also helps to consider anthropological evidence about the meaning of "manhood" or "masculinity" to develop a model, or conceptual definition, of gender. I draw the connections between gender and marriage for men and complete the development of the central thesis of *Marriage in Men's Lives*. Marriage is beneficial for men because of its meaning and implications for masculinity.

Earning Masculinity

All societies recognize and distinguish between males and females and have broadly understood institutionalized roles for adult men and women. Even in those rare societies in which a third, androgynous, category of gender exists, all individuals in all societies occupy a category and are expected to abide by prescribed rules. In our society, for example, stereotypical "ideals" serve as reference images against which all people are compared. We know this because there are "failures" at masculinity. Some men are viewed as insufficiently masculine, and we apply terms such as "effeminate," "unmanly," "sissy," or "emasculated" to them.

In other words, masculinity is more than an attribute that males possess automatically by virtue of their anatomy, age, or maturation; rather, it is something that must be attained or earned. At the same time, masculinity is indeed something that seems to be demanded of men, even of men who may not want it. For many purposes, a male must be sufficiently masculine to receive full rights as a member of our society. Those who fail suffer consequences. At a minimum, the insufficiently masculine man will be the subject of ridicule and derision. He may also be excluded from certain groups, denied access to some jobs, rejected as a potential suitor by women, or otherwise considered deviant. This aspect of masculinity appears to be almost universal. As comparative anthropologist David Gilmore (1990) notes, "This recurrent notion that manhood is problematic, a critical threshold that boys must pass through testing, is found at all levels of sociocultural development regardless of what other alternative roles are recognized. It is found among the simplest hunters and fishermen, among peasants and sophisticated urbanized peoples; it is found in all continents and environments. It is found among both warrior peoples and those who have never killed in anger" (Gilmore, 1990: 11).

Those men who fail the various tests of masculinity are judged according to their status *as males*. It is their actual gender identity that is called into question. They are not "real *men*." For a man to have his masculinity called into question is a serious challenge with potentially important consequences. In this respect, masculinity differs from femininity. Women are certainly judged by standards of sexual propriety and morality. But when they fail, it is not their status *as women* that is called into question so much as their claims to be moral, proper, or otherwise good people (Gilmore, 1990). With the exception of derogatory terms sometimes applied to lesbians, our language lacks commonly used words to describe the insufficiently feminine woman, yet abounds in those for the insufficiently masculine male. The importance of masculinity for a man's identity has implications for how it is experienced and how it is "displayed."

We tend to think of gender as a single concept or dimension with two complementary versions: male and female. However, it helps to view masculinity and femininity as different concepts rather than different points on the same dimension. Masculinity differs from femininity in at least one significant and fundamental way. *Men must continually prove and demonstrate their masculinity, whereas women do not need to constantly justify their claims to their femininity.*

To illuminate this distinction, let me begin with an important observation made by the French feminist psychologist Elisabeth Badinter in *XY: On Masculine Identity* (1995). As she notes, "The order so often heard—'Be a Man'—implies that it does not go without saying and that manliness may not be as natural as one would like to think. Being a man implies a labor, an effort that does not seem to be demanded of a woman. It is rare to hear the words 'Be a Woman' as a call to order, whereas the exhortation to the little boy, the male adolescent, or even the male adult is common in most societies" (1995: 1–2).

Even while the demand that boys and adult males "be men" is made, no clearly defined rites or rituals exist in contemporary American society by which males may do so. How is the male to become a "real man"? By which means and actions is he to accomplish this? By asking these questions, I am proposing that there *is*, in fact, insistence that it happen. In short, I am suggesting that, among the various responses a boy may make to the demand "act like a man," the least acceptable one would be the response "I don't want to." Acting like a man is part of the youthful script for boys and adult males. Some may not wish to and others may choose not to. Indeed, many boys may not wish to, even while they accede to the demands. Those who do not, however (i.e., those males who do not act, or try to act, like men), will pay for their deviance.

A number of psychologists, anthropologists, and sociologists have suggested that the development of a boy's gender identity is quite distinct from the development of a girl's femininity (Elisabeth Badinter, 1992; Nancy Chodorow, 1973; Erik Erikson, 1950; David Gilmore,1990; Ralph Greenson, 1968; Liam Hudson and Bernadine Jacot, 1991; Robert Stoller, 1985). To understand, begin with the basic idea that in order to develop an identity, individuals develop both a positive relation of *inclusion* and a negative relation of *exclusion*, a premise introduced by psychologist Erik Erikson (1950). The identity is formed by both processes. "One defines oneself by one's resemblances to some people and one's differences from others" (Badinter, 1995: 31). Alternatively, identity is formed through identification *and* differentiation. Boys do not develop identities *as* boys through positive identification with males only. They develop such identities through the joint processes of identification with males and the differentiation from females. This basic process of dual identification and differentiation, most now believe, is true for both boys and girls.

The difference between the sexes arises because of the nature of gestation and infant care. A boy is born to a woman. And in almost all cases, he is initially cared for by a woman. This prosaic fact—that a boy is born to a woman, nourished and cared for by a person of the opposite sex—has consequences for the development of masculinity in ways that do not pertain to girls and femininity. The intense unity that exists between a baby boy and his mother has different implications from the unity that exists between a baby girl and her mother. To become a man, a boy must differentiate himself from his mother and deny the mother-child unity of infancy. For a girl, however, the process is different. The early unity with the mother is consistent with a girl's identity as a woman. Her dependence on her mother is part of an identification that will be the basis of her own identity. Greenson (1968) was the first to note that if a boy is to identify with his father, he must first differentiate himself, imaginatively, from his mother, a process he called "disidentification." Once done, a boy may go on to identify with his father, a process Greenson called "counter-identification." Much of what I discuss as the "tests" that establish masculinity may be seen as part of the differentiation process that boys go through in the long path they travel to becoming "real men." In a sense, masculinity is defined in opposition to the dependencies of childhood on the mother. Masculinity, that is, is *not* femininity.

At some point in the first few years of life, and depending on the culture, a little boy is expected to establish an identity separate from his mother. As he begins to move around on his own, to explore and manipulate toys and objects, and to speak, he separates physically and psychologically from his mother. A little girl follows a similar path. It is at this stage, however, that a boy faces a special problem. For him, the sense of being a separate individual also involves the idea of being a different gender. He must create a sense of separateness that is qualitatively distinct from his mother because he is not a female as she is.

As sociologist Nancy Chodorow has noted, a little girl's femininity is consistent with, and reinforced by, her dependence on her mother. The opposite is true for the little boy:

> A boy, in his attempt to gain an elusive masculine identification, often comes to define this masculinity largely in negative terms, as that which is not feminine or involved with women. There is an internal and external aspect to this. Internally, the boy tries to reject his mother and deny his attachment to her and the strong dependence upon her that he still feels. He also tries to deny the deep personal identification with her that has developed during his early years. He does this by repressing whatever he takes to be feminine inside himself, and importantly, by denigrating and devaluing whatever he considers to be feminine in the outside world. (1973: 50)

Elisabeth Badinter develops this basic idea to show how masculinity is a task, or an *acquired* identity (1995: 67). As she notes, preadolescent boys must be "made" into men by various means. Childhood is left behind, and the boy is transformed into a young man. The young girl, in most cultures, *becomes* a young woman at menarche. Menstruation lays the basic foundation for the possibility of adult womanhood. No such thing happens for boys. The development of masculinity almost always involves "tests" of strength, endurance of pain, and independence. In many cultures, these initiation rites structure the gradual transition for boys to men. The almost complete absence of such rites in modern American society has important implications for how masculinity is "achieved."

Whether there are actual ritualized tests or rites for boys or not, all who successfully navigate the course to manhood pass a test of sorts, nonetheless. Every boy whose primary infant attachment was to his mother (this would include virtually all boys except those raised by men from birth) must succeed in breaking his primary tie to his mother *and* her gender. He must succeed in moving beyond the mother-child unity and establish himself as an independent individual with a different sexual identity.

If we assume, as most psychologists do, that the primary attachment to the mother, and the pleasures associated with it, must be rejected with difficulty, then we may also assume that some tension or wish to return to or restore them endures, at least in fantasy. The challenges for young boys (i.e., the assumption of a more complete independence from the mother) require something much more difficult than the passive dependence and symbiotic unity of early childhood. "In this view, the struggle for masculinity is a battle against these regressive wishes and fantasies, a hard-fought renunciation of the longings for the prelapsarian idyll of childhood" (Gilmore, 1990: 29).

Anthropologist David Gilmore applied this line of thought to the general similarity of masculine ideals that he discovered in his comparative research. He found the basic dimensions of masculinity to be relatively constant across cultures. However, the rigidity and severity or intensity of the male ideal varied with modes of social organization and production. "The harsher the environment and the scarcer the resources, the more manhood is stressed as inspiration and goal" (Gilmore, 1990: 224). Once we assume that most societies, for whatever reason, allocate reproductive and child-rearing tasks mainly to women, then the remaining imperative in all societies is productive tasks. This does not deny, of course, that women have historically been actively involved in the production and gathering of food. However, if men are not reproducers, they are relegated to productive tasks. Manhood, Gilmore argues, is a social construction to prevent regression to infantile dependencies by males. "Its critical threshold represents the point at which the boy produces more than he consumes and gives more than he takes. Manhood is the social barrier that societies must erect against entropy, human enemies, the forces of nature, time, and all the human weaknesses that endanger group life" (1990: 226).

This perspective portrays manhood as a social construction that moves males toward productivity and away from dependence, toward the acceptance of work and responsibility. Manhood fosters an orientation toward engagement with the real world, despite a reluctance to do so. Such a perspective on gender draws our attention to the ways in which social arrangements reinforce, again and again, adult masculinities. From childhood through adulthood, men are expected (i.e., it is normative) to maintain a demeanor that may often conflict with fantasy and actual desires. Social forces turn the male into a man and keep him that way. The effect of such force, what sociologists might call "social control" (normative barriers against deviance) becomes part of men's identities. At some point in most men's lives, the pressure to be masculine is no longer experienced as something that comes from others. Rather, the "desire" to act in ways consistent with the demands of masculinity seems rather natural and unexceptional. Masculinity becomes something men pursue as an end and not because they are being forced to. Social control becomes self-control.

Moreover, this view of masculinity makes it clear that it is not something a male "earns" and keeps. Instead, it is tenuous, potentially fleeting, and always at risk. The male, always confronted with the fantasy of infantile dependency and pleasurable symbiotic unity with his mother, must resist the regressive wish to be cared for, released from responsibility and action. This aspect of male identity, formed by dis-identification with the mother and counter-identification with the father, is what psychologists Hudson and Jacot (1995) refer to as "the male wound."

Being rooted in a primitive separation, the male's energies are in principle inexhaustible. They will last as long as his wound lasts . . . [for] the wound is not just an introduction to the experience of agency. It is an *energy source*, fueling symbolically significant action—typically in fields distant from mothers and fathers, sex and gender. The defining characteristic of such activity is that it is pursued with passion; not for extraneous reasons like profit or status, but as an end in itself. (1995: 49).

In the search for the meaning of manhood we must keep these two possibilities in mind: first, masculinity is earned by accomplishing things that are not female; second, there is no critical juncture at which point males may proclaim their masculinity as secure and "earned." The pursuit of masculinity will continue in men's lives. As helpful as these psychological insights are, they do not go far enough. We may assume that masculinity is defined in opposition to femininity (or maternity). And we may assume that this is an ongoing project for most males. But this process does not simply happen. Something drives it. To understand that force, we must return to the world of social relations and normative expectations. For it is here that we will find the source of the energy that drives the masculinizing process.

It is important to remember that the goal is to identify the "oughts" of adult masculinity. By this, I mean that we are not attempting to catalogue all differences between men and women. Instead, we must answer this question: what must men do to establish their claim to be men? A brief digression will clarify what this means. To illustrate the point, consider the question of men's aggressiveness, a trait that has been consistently associated with men more than women. Most males are more aggressive than most females. But not all, and certainly not always. The real question, therefore, is whether men must be aggressive to maintain their claims to be men.

Aggression per se is not a core element of masculinity. However, men may be required to be aggressive to be masculine. We can resolve this apparent contradiction by focusing on certain *roles* that define masculinity rather than certain *traits*. For men to demonstrate and retain their claim to masculine status, they are expected to occupy certain culturally defined roles. Such roles are understood through their objectives, and in their pursuit, men may be required to be aggressive or, perhaps, even submissive. Some personality traits, that is, should be seen as secondary elements of social roles that may demand them. Aggression is not a social role. Rather, it is a trait found in many men. So, if men tend to be more aggressive than women, the sociological explanation for this pattern is found in the requirements of adequate role performance. What social roles are men expected to occupy that are likely to produce or demand aggressiveness? The point is that we must shift our focus from the psychological to the sociological, from personality to social structure, from traits to roles.

What about the possibility that aggression is somehow "programmed" in men, that it may reside in biochemistry or genetic makeup? Men may have whatever it takes to be more aggressive *because* of these components. And they may have many other traits, as well. These components they may, or may not, share with females. Yet such an observation is relatively unimportant for this argument because the "inherent" source of any trait does not adequately explain its expression. Suppose that musical talent inheres in genes. The child who is lucky enough to inherit such genes will not automatically become a musician any more than the child who inherits whatever it takes to be aggressive will necessarily behave that way. Something else must happen for potentials to be displayed. And that something, surely, is elaborated by the relationships one has with other people. In fact, aggression may be "produced" in men by particular configurations of social relationships. Various patterns of hierarchical relationships may evoke more or less aggressive responses by men (Kruez and Rose, 1972; Kruez, Rose, and Jennings, 1972).

Continuing with this question about aggression and masculinity, we should again ask whether a male could sustain his claim to manhood *without* demonstrating aggression? Can there be such a thing as a nonaggressive man? Is aggression actually optional as part of the masculine script? The answer is that it depends on how a man executes the social roles that actually define his masculinity. If, by some means or the other, he is able to adequately perform without being aggressive, then the answer to these questions is "Yes." The fact that men are generally more aggressive than women, however, suggests that such an accomplishment is difficult or beyond most men.

All of this leads us to the final question about how to define masculinity: what are the roles that males are expected to assume in order to validate their masculinity? Comparative anthropology offers some guidance. Gender, unlike marriage, is fairly stable from one society to another, at least with respect to men. Indeed, the image of manhood, though not universal, appears quite general. As Gilmore notes, "These gender ideals . . . differ from one culture to another. But . . . underlying the surface differences are some intriguing similarities among cultures that otherwise display little in common. Most social scientists would agree that there do exist striking regularities in standard male and female roles across cultural boundaries regardless of other social arrangements" (1990: 10).

Gilmore's research used a sample of cultures that included hunting-gathering bands, horticultural and pastoral tribes, peasants and industrial civilizations, and peoples from all inhabited continents. He included warrior and pacifist societies; matrilineal, patrilineal, and bilateral kinship systems; and those known for their rigid gender-based stratification, as well as those generally viewed as more egalitarian. Other anthropologists have come to similar conclusions (e.g., Gregor, 1985; Tolson, 1977; Williams and Best, 1990). Drawing on such sources, we may define masculinity by the following three social roles. Throughout the world, males are expected to assume at least three roles to be complete members of adult society:

1. *Fathers to Their Wives' Children.* Masculinity and fatherhood are closely related throughout the world. "Real men" are variously described by reference to their testicles: "a man with big testicles," "well endowed with testicles," or "much cojones [balls]" (Gilmore, 1990: 41). Sexual potency and prowess, however, are not sufficient anywhere to warrant a claim to adult masculinity. Men must also be able to produce children. And it is husbands who are expected to accomplish this. When a married couple is childless, the blame in most of the world's cultures is placed on the man (1990: 42). And, as noted in the last chapter, no society has ever approved of childbearing outside of marriage. Thus, men must be sexually "successful" in producing children. And since children are expected (everywhere) to be born to a married woman, this means that men must be married fathers.

2. *Providers for Their Families.* Throughout the world, fathers are held responsible for providing for their wives and children. The man who is *unable*, because of illness or inability, to do so may incur the pity of others. But the man who is *unwilling* to do so incurs more than pity. He is scorned and vilified. He has not accepted his responsibility as an adult member of society. Men are supposed to work, even when they might prefer not to, to provide adequate support for their dependents and, often, to provide a legacy or patrimony to be inherited.

3. *Protectors of Their Wives and Children.* When necessary, a man is expected to stand up for his family, to show courage and loyalty to them. He is expected to defend his pride, his honor, his "name" and that of his family. And with respect to more formal types of protection, men are always responsible for military defense, even when women may participate in warfare. No society relies principally on females to be the soldiers or warriors.

This trinity of social roles defines masculinity in an inherently sociological and anthropological way. It focuses attention on those things that men are expected to be. And it is in the performance of these roles that men may become aggressive, assertive, competitive, hierarchical, or any number of other things commonly (or stereotypically) associated with them and the way they act and think.

In their cross-cultural research on sex stereotypes, Williams and Best (1990) found that there are, in fact, very broad similarities in those traits associated with the roles that men typically occupy. In their research they asked a small sample of students in each of 30 countries to respond to 300 adjectives by indicating whether each was more frequently associated with men than women, or vice versa. The adjectives found to be associated with men were grouped into the following headings:

1. *Dominance*—seeking leadership roles in groups and being influential and controlling in individual relationships
2. *Autonomy*—acting independently of others or of social values and expectations
3. *Aggression*—engaging in behaviors that attack or hurt others

4. *Exhibition*—behaving in such a way as to elicit the immediate attention of others
5. *Achievement*—striving to be outstanding in pursuits of socially recognized significance
6. *Endurance*—persisting in any task undertaken (1990: 228)

The similarity that these researchers found among societies in the traits typically associated with men is a clear reflection of the similarity of roles that men occupy around the world. So, if men are generally thought to be more dominant than women, this is a reflection of men's roles as fathers, providers, and protectors. In those roles, presumably, men are called upon to be dominant to perform adequately. Likewise, aggression or achievement are traits that may be understood as part of being an adequate father, provider, and protector.

The advantage of such an approach is that it allows for subtle, as well as very obvious, differences in the meaning of *manhood*. At different times and in different places, the influence of events may alter the magnitude and importance of the injunction to "be a man." Warfare, economic depressions, religious movements, racial and ethnic values, and many other such cultural events and patterns may produce variations in what is expected of men. Still, the variations revolve around common themes that do not appear to change very much, even when it becomes more or less difficult for men to enact them. The times may make the core dimensions of masculinity more or less important than other social goals (especially warfare), so it is not surprising that the social pressure to assume each role (father, provider, protector) is variable over time.

There may even be some men who are able to refuse to comply with the social commandments of manhood, at least for a time. And presumably, there will always be those who are willing or eager to refuse to comply. But to repeat a point I made in the first chapter: strong social norms are sometimes violated by some, but never violated by most.

To find that masculinity is broadly defined by the roles men occupy as husbands, fathers, and protectors alerts us to the centrality of marriage in men's lives. And yet, such a definition of "masculinity" explains only part of the dynamics of the process. How does marriage sustain masculinity? What about marriage matters? And most important, what connects the social institution of marriage to the adult male so as to define him as masculine?

Connecting Marriage and Masculinity

Marriage is one of the most basic and necessary requirements for adult masculinity, although not sufficient alone. Marriage is so closely connected with assumptions about adult males that men deemed to have failed the cultural tests of their gender identity are often denied the right to marry.

For example, among the East African Samburu tribe (relatives of the Masai) studied by Paul Spencer (1965), males go through a series of well-defined age strata consisting of boy, young man (moran), and elder. During the middle stage, boys must pass a number of tests and go through rituals that culminate in social recognition of their adult masculinity. The first such ritual is the test of circumcision. Without any form of anesthetic, this operation takes place in front of the boy's male relatives and prospective in-laws. A boy must remain absolutely motionless and silent during the entire procedure. Should he flinch or cry out, he may not be allowed to progress to the next step toward adulthood. The successful boy then goes on to other tests and preparations for adult male status, mainly involving cattle husbandry. One of the final tests during the middle stage of life requires a young man to kill an ox and distribute the meat. Once this is done, the young man moves to the adult stage of full manhood (*lee*; Spencer, 1965: 107–8). No man is allowed to marry, however, until he kills his first ox. Marriage, in short, is reserved only for those who have passed all tests of adult manhood, especially proof of being an effective provider (i.e., a hunter).

The same general pattern is found among the New Guinea Sambia, detailed by anthropologist Gilbert Herdt (1981). Boys must endure painful ordeals on their way to manhood. They must also acquit themselves as good hunters. Those who do not are denied the privilege of marriage and are scorned by women. And those who are exceptionally good hunters may have several wives (1981: 83). The !Kung bushmen of southwest Africa, likewise, reserve marriage only for those males who have shown themselves adequate in tests of their masculinity—in this case killing an antelope (Marshall, 1976: 170).

There are no comparable restrictions on American men. But neither are there ritualistic markers of masculinity in this society. At what point is a young male a man? In the absence of ritualized transitions or other clearly defined points in the life course that establish a legitimate claim to masculinity, the focus should shift to marriage itself. Is marriage a rite of passage into manhood? Does marriage (in our society) establish the minimum claims to adult masculinity that are subsequently reinforced and displayed in other ways? As I suggest here, marriage may be viewed just this way. The young husband is a different social and legal person than he was as a bachelor. He is held to different standards. He is accorded different treatment by friends, family, associates, and strangers. He may legitimately claim greater autonomy and respect than before he married. He has made a public commitment of the most enduring and binding sort. He expects to be treated as mature, stable, productive, and dependable. He has made a public statement about his sexual orientation and does not need to defend it. He has competed in a contest and won the affections of a woman over all other men. His wife has sworn to forgo all others for him. He has succeeded in courtship. He is now a husband and, in certain respects, he is now a "man." Or at least he has established the most minimal right to make such a claim.

But masculinity is precarious and a marriage does little more than lay the foundation for it. The husband must also sustain and promote his claim to masculinity. And it is in his marriage that he will be able to do that. In fact, it is difficult to imagine how he might do so well as a man without being married.

To understand how marriage reinforces and sustains masculinity, it is useful to consider a gender model that allows us to see how marriage matters. Hudson and Jacot's research (1995), reported in *The Way Men Think*, attempts to explain why men and women think, imagine, and act differently, although that is not my purpose here. The authors provide a gender model that I use to connect marriage and masculinity.

Hudson and Jacot suggest that gender should be viewed as a dynamic process rather than a single binary distinction. Men and women *construct* their genders through a series of actions and decisions that cumulatively define them as more or less masculine, more or less feminine. The gender model involves four levels, each of which contains two possibilities, male and female: (1) biology, anatomy, and physiology; (2) gender identity; (3) object choice; and (4) presentation of self. As the authors note, "It is from these four facets of maleness or femaleness that the personality of each individual is composed—and sometimes recomposed" (1995: 21).

Biology, Anatomy, and Physiology

As a result of anatomy (physical differences in genitalia, size, musculature, etc.) males and females look, and possibly act, differently. Parents and others respond to such differences in predictable ways. Little boys are treated differently than little girls in obvious and subtle ways: their dress, their play, the expectations about them, and the behaviors sanctioned. In short, biology establishes certain bases on which others, especially parents, act. Such biological differences are "the raw material on which the institutions of a particular culture set to work—and chief among those institutions is the family" (Hudson and Jacot, 1995: 25). Gender includes a biological dimension that most people call "sex," as in "which sex is the newborn?" Though rooted in biology, such anatomical factors figure very importantly in our notions of gender (i.e., "maleness" or "femaleness").

Gender Identity

Here the question is about one's own sense of belonging either to the male or the female half of the species. Most children have a sketchy sense of this by 18 months of age. And for most adults, gender identity is stable. However, as Hudson and Jacot advise, the sense of being male or female is not always a clean distinction, even for adult men or women: "A man may experience himself as unambiguously male on the football pitch, yet as genderless, even 'female,' when making love. A woman may experience herself as genderless, even 'male,' while selling life insurance, but as un-ambiguously female when she bathes her child. Our framework must make space, in other words, for people whose sense of their own maleness or femaleness is intermittent or subject to local reversals" (1995: 25–26). In their ordinary lives, people's behaviors create a personal sense of gender; we experience ourselves as more or less masculine or feminine as we negotiate experience and relationships with others. How an individual imaginatively experiences himself or herself may, or may not, always agree with what others see. In fantasy or imagination, individuals may be considerably less "fixed" as males or females than the image they project. In imagination, at least, men and women may travel long distances between the poles of masculinity and femininity as times and circumstances change.

Object Choice

Our object choice is the person on whom we find our erotic passions focused. Such a choice is more than a particular individual. Rather, it pertains to a *class* of individuals, the same sex or the opposite sex, similar to ourselves in personality and social background, or different. As Hudson and Jacot note, the combination of gender identity and object-choice possibilities creates such interesting prospects as a "male lesbian." "A man who sees himself as a man and is drawn to women is making a choice of like-with-unlike, the conventional pattern. But if he sees himself as a woman and is attracted to women, there is a significant respect in which he is not heterosexual but a 'lesbian'" (1995: 27). The combinations of gender identity and object choice may produce patterns that defy clean definition by traditional "male-female" logic. Yet once it is acknowledged that object choice means more than whether we are attracted solely to those of the same or different sex, that object choice also refers to gender identity of the other person, it is likely that circumstances will conspire to produce combinations of gender identity and object choice that are neither unambiguously masculine nor feminine—or at least occasionally it will be so.

Presentation of Self

Here the focus is on culturally defined methods of behaving and presenting oneself to others. Men and women are expected to act and think differently to varying degrees. Such expectations arise in matters of jobs (kindergarten teacher for men; automobile mechanic for women) clothing (skirts for men, neckties for women), speech and mannerisms, to name but a few obvious arenas for the presentation of self. Some degree of conformity to convention is the result of such normative expectations. The *degree* of conformity, of course, is another matter. Stereotypical images of men and women influence individual's behaviors and aspirations. Such stereotypes also influence reactions to other people.

Each of the four dimensions may be thought to embody at least two possible options—one "male" and the other "female." The combination of all four results in a particular pattern, of which 16 are possible. Two, in particular, are stereotypically known: the male, who perceives himself as a man, desires women and presents himself in a masculine light; and the female, who sees herself as a woman, desires men and presents herself as feminine (1995: 33).

People do not always present or experience themselves as completely and unambiguously "male" or "female," however. Instead, it is more likely that elements of both exist in the presentation and sense of self. What, for example, are we to make of men who dress as males ordinarily do, but who wear items of women's jewelry (e.g., pierced earrings)? This affectation combines, however slightly, the customary female with the customary male modes of dress. In short, this model of gender embodies the common sense possibility that masculinity exists in shades and degrees. It accords with a view of masculinity as tentative and possibly fleeting, because men may make different choices on various dimensions in different circumstances.

At the same time, the levels of gender coalesce into relatively consistent patterns. There is little reason to believe that a heterosexual man would become homosexual in fantasy or behavior without some dramatic external pressure (e.g., the complete absence of female companionship for years on end). Such an event would make little sense. However, some homosexuals do, at some point, "come out." They decide to alter their presentation of self to accord with their gender identity and object choice. This is the more interesting event because it suggests that something about these gender dimensions typically produces a consistent and coherent pattern. A more or less stable pattern characterizes most adult men (and women), even when minor variations are possible and even likely. How such a stable configuration is constructed and maintained is the issue. How does a man create a system of gender dimensions that is consistently and stably masculine? To answer this question, we need to return to the normative definition of marriage developed in the last chapter.

Normative marriage is one framework and foundation that supports and sustains an adult man's masculinity. The various dimensions and characteristics that define marriage also support and define masculinity. In their adult married roles, men continually define and reveal themselves as masculine. Now reconsider the dimensions of normative marriage in light of the model of gender just presented. In the following discussion, I presume that sex (the first of the four dimensions of gender) is fixed, making gender identity, object choice, and presentation of self the three dimensions subject to definition or affirmation.

Gender Identity

Here the question is which aspects of normative marriage are likely to be associated with the *sense* of being more or less male. Recall that the underlying theme of gender identity for men is separation from the mother. It is the passive closeness of the mother-child relationship that is rejected as the boy develops his identity as a male. The antithesis of close, expressive, personal, passive comfort with the mother is formal, impersonal, agency—in short, a world governed by rules and standards, where the man is responsible not dependent, active, not passive. In the world of work and enforced adult responsibilities masculine identity is easily developed, sustained, and displayed.

Here the normative expectation that men should be the primary breadwinners of their families ("Husband as Head") is most obviously relevant. In his role as earner of most family income, the husband is subordinate to the impersonal world of economic matters. The traditional husband submits to the rules of advancement in his job and career—for the sake of his family. The impersonal and hierarchical nature of productive pursuits is the antithesis of child-like passivity. Normative marriage venerates such pursuits. Indeed, it demands them. The husband *must be a provider* because there are no accepted legitimate alternatives. Husbands cannot easily choose to be homemakers. Instead, married men work and earn, thereby constructing a masculine identity.

Marriage also affirms the antithesis of infantile dependency by celebrating maturity. As noted earlier, there is no marker in our lives by which we may examine ourselves and declare "now I am mature." Marriage, however, is associated with notions of maturity and thus confers some amount of legitimacy to such a claim. In their married roles as fathers, providers, and protectors, husbands validate themselves as mature men.

Object Choice

By his marriage, a man has declared his heterosexual object choice by binding himself to an institution that presumes and insists upon it. More important, since marriage in America is based on love and free choice, the union is typically the culmination of a "successful" courtship conducted on the two partners' own terms. Marriage, therefore, is a decision informed by real experience with a person of the opposite sex. The importance of this point should not be minimized. One can imagine many reasons for marriage: the consolidation of family names or estates, the creation or maintenance of political alliances, or the need for minimal economic security, to name only three. Historically, such reasons for marriage were regarded as legitimate and involved family elders in important ways. And, historically, premarital courtship was surrounded by formal codes of decorum and propriety. It is quite safe to assume that unmarried couples today enjoy vastly greater amounts of privacy, intimacy, and freedom than their forebears did. Dating, the conventional method of mate selection, is imbued with heavy doses of romantic love and eroticism. A marriage is the result of a decision on the part of the couple to recognize the "success" of such endeavors and experiences. In the virtual absence of other reasons for marriage, love means that the two partners are convinced and certain about their erotic attraction to one another. And such conviction is usually born of experience. The virgin bride or groom is a distinct statistical exception today. In 1995, Laumann et al. reported that 16% of men and 30% of women were virgins at their wedding. If we look only at younger Americans born since World War II, these percentages are even lower. For men and women under age 50, only 15% of men and 20% of women report being virgins when they married (Laumann et al., 1995: 503).

Other aspects of normative marriage sustain heterosexuality. The strong norm of marital fidelity establishes a reciprocal ownership of each partner's sexuality; he "owns" hers and she "owns" his. Each has sole claim on the other and no person may legitimately transgress these property boundaries. Marriage limits sexual access. It restricts choice in very obvious ways. Married spouses have voluntarily accepted these borders. Husbands are not allowed by custom or law to pursue other sexual partners. To do so would be to violate the strongest of marriage rules. So, while the decision to marry may be viewed as the successful consequence of a heterosexual relationship with a particular woman, the fidelity rule enforces that decision so long as the marriage endures. And so does the rule of monogamy. Monogamous marriages elevate the notion of sexual fidelity to its peak, restricting one's sexual partner completely. It should be recalled that the idea of object choice pertains to the type of person one finds arousing. Even within the broad outlines of heterosexual others, there is a wide range of choices based on issues of personality, physical appearance, and social characteristics. Together, the two rules of fidelity and monogamy eliminate, or at least suspend, all other options so long as the marriage lasts.

This last point warrants brief consideration. Object choice is arguably the most conspicuous feature of American marriage. As I noted previously, since love is its foundation and premise, a marriage succeeds or fails mostly because of the compatibility of partnerships. Staying together presumes such compatibility. And when one or the other spouse discovers that he or she desires a different "type" of partner, the marriage typically ends. This is well-known, and the recognized reason for divorce in our society. But there is something about this well-known fact that is less well appreciated. If couples "fall out of love," or come to find other persons sufficiently more alluring and attractive to justify ending their marriages, then this must mean that object choice, in the most general sense of that term, is not completely stable. Indeed, if it were, there would be little reason for norms and laws about fidelity. Because such rules are institutionalized as core elements of marriage, there is probably some reason for them.

Presentation of Self

The final issue pertains to questions about the role of marriage in structuring the way husbands present themselves as men. Here the focus is on those dimensions of normative marriage that contribute to an open and public image that announces and sustains masculinity.

The most obvious place to begin is with the normative expectation that husbands be fathers. As I noted in the last chapter, marriage establishes a social connection between a man and his wife's children. Married men accept an enduring obligation to provide for and protect any children born into the union. In fact, the primary difference between a married and an unmarried father is this public quality of the voluntary assumption of abiding responsibility. By law and custom, married fathers become accountable to others for the adequate care of children born to their wives. Failure to do so is much more than a moral fault. It is the occasion for civil sanctions. So, whereas fatherhood is undoubtedly a marker of adult masculinity, it is legitimately so only in the context of marriage. By marrying the woman who bears his (or, presumably his) children, a man has established a legitimate claim to adult manhood.

Likewise, the norm that holds husbands to be the head of the household, the breadwinner, and primary income earner contributes to a very public manifestation of adult masculinity. This is illustrated by the husband who does not provide for his wife (and children). As I noted earlier, when men become dependent on their wives, behavioral manifestations result that reveal how strongly provision is associated with masculinity in our collective views. Such men, it will be recalled, increasingly withdraw from "traditional" feminine responsibilities such as child care and homemaking to compensate for their "failures" (Brines, 1994). Husbands are *supposed* to work, earn, and provide. So, if they do not, what are they? Certainly much more than poor providers. In a real sense, such men are not adequate husbands.

This is an old idea. In fact, it was a key element in the description of the "functional nuclear family" written in the mid-1950s. Sociologists of the time argued that husbands and fathers occupy "instrumental," wives and mothers "expressive" positions in the family. For the man, this distinction means that he is primarily involved in the public world of work and civic affairs (Parsons and Bales, 1955). Whether such a division of marriage roles is actually related to the efficient functioning of a nuclear family, as many argued, is not the point. Rather, the association of men with work and provision for the family is the issue. Men as husbands, then as now, have been engaged in earning the income and providing for the household, in short, conforming to public standards of what it means to be an adult man.

So far, I have attempted to connect the elements of normative marriage with a rudimentary model of gender. My point is simple. In their marriages, and by their marriages, men define and display themselves as masculine. Marriage is one social arrangement that both creates and reproduces gender. As Berk (1985) rightly claimed, the family is the *gender factory*. Recalling the three basic social roles that define masculinity in all of the world's cultures, we see the centrality of marriage. As fathers to their wives' children, providers and protectors of them, men resolve the persisting challenges of sustaining and displaying their masculinity. The marriages that men and women create are environments for masculine identity and expression. They may also be an important arena for the expression of feminine identity. And the normative boundaries that surround marriage foster that masculinity. Marriage, for men, is an ongoing enterprise of self-definition, presentation of self, and choice of partner. The soft boundaries around marriages strengthen, reinforce, and refine the consistency of the options that, together, produce gender. By providing options within a narrow range, and by calling for behaviors of a certain type, the expectations of normative marriage also reinforce and build masculine identities. In this sense, normative marriage is a masculinity template. As we continue to pursue the guiding question of *Marriage in Men's Lives*, I will rely on this perspective. When we ask why marriage appears to be beneficial to men, one possible answer is that the institution of marriage, at least in its most traditional form, is a socially approved mechanism for the expression of masculinity.

Measures of Normative Marriage

If this argument is correct, marriage would imply something about how men direct their energies, express themselves, and otherwise establish themselves as men. If we assume that all men are expected to establish and maintain their masculinity (an assumption supported by evidence already presented), then it follows that marriage will have consistent and predictable consequences. Moreover, more traditional marriages will have different consequences from less traditional ones. To investigate such possibilities, I follow two strategies. First, I assess men before and after they marry. Second, I consider how married men change in response to changes in their marriages. The argument asserts that there will be variations in men's behaviors to the extent that their marriages conform or depart from the normative model. Some marriages are simply less conventional than others, and men in such marriages will differ predictably from men in more traditional unions.

The dimensions of normative marriage can be measured, even if incompletely. Together, these measures will provide a crude indicator of the extent of conventionality in the current marriage. Over time, marriages change as jobs come and go; babies are born, grow up, and leave home; and spouses adjust to one another's desires and quirks. Some of these changes make marriages more or less similar to the model of normative marriage outlined earlier. When marriages vary from that model, there should be consistent and corresponding changes in men's lives. If so, then the idea that marriage sustains and reinforces traditional masculine behaviors gains credibility.

In the next chapter I describe the measures of free choice, maturity, parenthood, husband as head, and fidelity that are the indicators of normative marriage.

The balance of *Marriage in Men's Lives* investigates how these factors explain men's behaviors in a wide range of settings. Before turning to that effort, however, I must explain which aspects of men's lives will be investigated. What are the expected outcomes resulting from variations in free choice, maturity, headship, fidelity, and parenthood (i.e., what are the dependent variables)?

In what ways would marriage change men, and how do men in "strongly" normative marriages (as defined above) differ from those in less conventional unions? Undoubtedly there are psychological and social-psychological consequences that could be explored (see Hudson and Jacot, 1995). Married men, for example, might enjoy better health, both mental and otherwise, because of something intangible about marriage. They may think and imagine differently, for example, once they are married or once they become fathers. Such possibilities, though interesting, are secondary. The most relevant questions about married men pertain to their public lives. But I do not mean only what happens outside the home. Instead, I am referring to those aspects of men's lives that take place outside the psychological realm—in their communities, their families, their jobs. In short, I am interested in married men's behaviors rather than their thoughts and dreams.

Now it becomes much easier to anticipate the consequences of marriage in men's lives. In particular, as fathers, providers, and protectors, married men differ from unmarried men (1) in their adult *achievement,* (2) in involvement, participation, and engagement in *social life* and *organizations,* and (3) in expressions of *generosity* or philanthropy.

Adult achievement. To begin with the simplest prediction, married men should achieve more than unmarried men. Providing for the family is such a central part of normative marriage and masculinity that otherwise comparable men should have different adult attainments as a result of their marital histories. Once they marry, men will do better in their jobs. They will earn and work more. Achievement in the world is central to masculine gender identity. Marriage supports the earnest pursuit of achievement in America. Indeed, marriage venerates such pursuits. Moreover, differences among married men reflect the various dimensions of marriage outlined above. When two otherwise similar married men are compared, the one married longer should have achieved more, for example, just as the one with children versus the one without.

Social participation. Married men should be more highly involved in certain organizations and more likely to participate in some types of civic affairs. Social participation is a form of gender display (presentation of self) for men. Generally, high levels of engagement and involvement in public as opposed to private matters is consistent with the logic of the masculine image. Men who eschew public life, who retreat into the private worlds of their families, are not openly demonstrating their masculinity. Rather, the world of private affairs, family life, home, and children is the principal domain of women. If masculine identity is defined in opposition to such things, we would expect to find displays of this in the form of open involvement in public life.

More specifically, the type of involvement that marriage is likely to foster is in groups governed by clearly defined rules of membership. Masculine involvement with others is likely to be organized by membership in a defined *role*. For this reason, marriage is likely to lead to greater involvement in organizations such as churches or job-related groups in which participation is governed by clearly defined rules and standards. On the other hand, marriage may actually reduce involvement in very informal, personal relationships such as those with friends or casual contacts.

Generosity. Acts of generosity are direct extensions of the marital roles of provider and protector. The philanthropist is assisting others, providing for their needs and protecting against misfortune. The generous philanthropist is engaging in an act that mirrors what Veblen called "conspicuous consumption." He is engaging in "conspicuous provision." Only the anonymous donor might be said to be motivated solely by moral principles of generosity, and even he may have other motives. Charities and foundations know this well and offer recognition in many ways as an incentive and inducement to giving. The man who is recognized for his gift is also recognized for his ability to give, for his productive abilities and successes. Philanthropic gifts, in short, are conspicuous displays of achievement.

As with social participation, however, marriage is likely to foster a certain *type* of giving and helping. In particular, married men's gifts are likely to be patterned by role expectations (i.e., norms). A married man is less likely to help out a friend and more likely to help his church or close relative.

Summary

The connection between marriage and masculinity is the key to understanding how and why men change when they get married. I began this chapter by arguing that masculinity is an ongoing project in men's lives. There is no point at which one may claim that he is now an adult male. Instead, masculinity must be continually built, sustained, and reinforced. And throughout the world, the core dimensions of adult masculinity include three distinct roles. Men must be (1) married fathers, (2) providers for, and (3) protectors of their wives and children. Adult masculinity is closely allied with marriage throughout the world.

I developed a way to view masculinity that includes several dimensions: gender identity, object choice, and presentation of self. Each of these dimensions of gender can vary between purely "male" and purely "female" poles. In gender identity, for example, a male may see himself more or less male, or more or less female. The same is true for object choice and presentation of self.

I then connected the dimensions of gender with the model of normative marriage developed in the last chapter to show how marriage supports and sustains masculinity. Masculinity and marriage are clearly connected. A man in a traditional marriage conforms to a strong masculine ideal: he has openly expressed his object choice (women). In his role as primary provider of the family, he has committed himself to instrumental tasks that contribute to his gender identity as a man (i.e., clearly not female). And as fathers, married men have publicly and openly accepted enduring and binding obligations. In and through their marriages, males may conform to a model of and express themselves as men. The question, therefore, is how?

When I considered the ways that marriage would change men, I drew directly from the foregoing connection with masculinity. The most obvious consequence of marriage is that men will provide for their families—a central assumption of adult masculinity. Married men will be more successful than unmarried men. Married men will also become more active in certain types of communities and organizations. They will see less of others with whom they have only an informal and personal connection and participate more in those contexts where they occupy roles governed by clear expectations. Finally, marriage will affect men's generosity by shifting their allegiances from informal friendships to more structured relationships based on well-defined expectations and obligations. These are the behavioral manifestations of marriage in men's lives. I take each up in the following three chapters.

4

Adult Achievement

Some of the most important influences in adult achievement are those over which individuals have little or no control. Each person is born with certain *ascribed characteristics* (e.g., race, sex, or family background) that influence opportunities and actual achievements. Other forces, however, are under an individual's control. People have some command over the amount of schooling they complete, for example. Or childbearing may be postponed until children are less likely to interfere with educational or occupational pursuits.

Like all societies, ours has a customary series of stages toward adulthood. Men are expected to finish basic schooling before entering the labor force, for example. But where does marriage figure into the process of adult achievement? The answer is that marriage is a critical step along the way to full adult status. It distinguishes the immature young man from the more stable mature husband. It is a public symbol that says much about a man. Employers value marriage and reward it. Marriage is also the engine that fuels greater effort and dedication to the goal of doing well.

My task in this and the following two chapters is to examine men's behavior to show how it is affected by marriage. In this chapter I examine whether men become more successful as a result of marriage. I also ask whether the various dimensions of normative marriage influence how much success married men enjoy. First, I examine the consequences of marriage by comparing men's lives before and after their marriages. Then I examine how variations in the normative dimensions of their marriages affect them. I examine whether male heads of families are more successful than men who share equally with their wives in the task of providing for their families and whether fathers are more successful than their married childless counterparts.

Measuring Achievement

The focus here is on *public* signs of achievement, or the aspects of success that take place outside of men's minds. The view of marriage as a component of masculinity directs attention to those tasks connected with providing for the family. Therefore, I will examine income, occupation, and work effort.

The research reported in this chapter is based on repeated annual interviews with the same 5,383 men who are part of a large nationally representative sample of Americans, the National Longitudinal Survey of Youth (NLSY). These men were between the ages of 14 and 21 in 1979 when they were first interviewed. Each year since, these men have been re-interviewed (the last year used in this research is 1993). Sponsored by the Bureau of Labor Statistics, U.S. Department of Labor, the NLSY is one of the most comprehensive and representative studies of young adults (both males and females) ever conducted.

There are a number of good reasons to use the NLSY to measure the consequences of marriage in men's lives. Because all men were 21 or younger when they were first interviewed, few were married. This makes it possible to follow a large group of men as they move through the early years of young adulthood. Rather than compare married with single men (as one might with a cross-sectional study), the NLSY permits an analysis of the *consequences* of marriage in each man's life. The few men who were already married at the beginning of the study (in 1979) are excluded from this research. All men in this work, therefore, began the study before ever marrying. By comparing various measures of achievement before and after marriage, we are actually studying the *changes* that occur. This important technical issue requires some elaboration.

The method used to analyze the NLSY in this chapter (a pooled cross-section time-series study with fixed effects) measures change in each man's life. Before-and-after data on men who married in the course of the study are compared. In order to conclude that marriage has an effect on men's achievements, individual men must *change* when they marry. If they do not, one cannot conclude that marriage had any effect.

The focus on *change* in men's lives is critical, because married and single men may differ in ways completely unrelated to marriage. Certainly, a man who never marries may be a different type from one who does—for example, a man may have a serious disability that limits his ability to find and attract a spouse. To the extent that such a disability also affects an unmarried man's achievements, then this man does indeed differ from a married man without such disabilities, but this difference derives from his disability status, not his marriage status.

To show that marriage (or some aspect of marriage) is the cause of achievement differences, three conditions must be met. First, there must be a correlation between the marital status of men (i.e., married or not) and their levels of achievement. Second, differences in marital status must temporally precede the differences in achievement. And finally, there must be no third factor that produces both the marital status differences and the achievement differences. If a disability limits a man's marriage potential *and* his achievements, that disability acts as a third factor responsible for the other two.

To completely rule out all such third factors when studying cause-effect relationships is not possible. However, if the same individuals are studied before and after marriage, and if there are consistent changes, such differences are likely the result of marriage rather than some other related factor. The strategy used for this analysis eliminates the confounding effects of most individual (i.e., third factor) traits related to both marriage and achievement. For example, African-American males have lower marriage rates than white men do. On average, minority males also earn less. But these relationships tell us nothing about the possible consequences of marriage for earnings. Perhaps black men's earnings are lower *because* they are less likely to marry. Alternatively, lower earnings may be the consequence of other behaviors and characteristics unrelated to marriage. If one were to compare black and white males, there would be a strong relationship between marital status and earnings. Again, such a relationship does not necessarily say anything about the causal connection between income and marriage.

If, however, black and white men are studied *before and after* marriage and incomes rise for *both* (regardless of age at the time of marriage), then assertions about the consequence of marriage are more plausible. It is still possible, of course, that the causal event was not marriage per se but some factor that routinely occurs at the same time as marriage. One can never completely rule out such possibilities, no matter how unlikely they may be.

The thoughtful reader will already have identified one possible flaw in this line of reasoning. As noted, the men in this research were all 21 or younger when they entered the study. Over the course of 15 years, as the study continued, these men aged. And it is well-known that achievement tends to rise with age, especially among young people in their midtwenties to late thirties. Some change in achievement levels, therefore, should be expected among these men *regardless* of their matrimonial histories. Fortunately, this is not the problem it might appear to be.

The question I ask is whether *changes in achievement* are greater in the presence of *changes in marital status* than in the absence of them. A young man's annual income may increase by an average of $500 per year regardless of whether he marries, but this research asks whether income increases more once he is married than it did when he wasn't. If not, then there is no imputed consequence of marriage.[1]

As a nationally representative sample, the NLSY represents the diversity of races, regions, and other characteristics found in America. Yet all comparisons are relative to a man's *own* levels of achievement before and after he married. Thus, even if men of different regions or races have differing incomes, such differences do not confound the results.[2]

Marital Status

The NLSY results appear in two sections. The first shows simple comparisons involving changes in marital status. Here the concern is whether changes in marital status itself can bring about changes in achievement. The second section, which follows, focuses attention on the married men only. In that section, I highlight various dimensions of normative marriage and ask if men's achievements are affected by variations in their marriages. Throughout the chapter, I consider three measures of achievement: annual income, annual weeks worked, and occupational prestige.

The first set of graphs presents the consequences of changes in marital status for each of the three measures of achievement. The line drawn across the middle of each graph represents "no change" in the measure considered. Positive changes will appear above the line, and negative changes below it. The changes represented in these graphs occurred in addition to any associated with age. That is, the typical changes in achievement associated with aging have been removed before I examined the consequences of marriage. The effects shown for marital status changes, therefore, are not influenced by the fact that marriage typically occurs in a man's late twenties or early thirties.

To illustrate, consider Figure 4.1, which deals with annual income. The bar for marriage is drawn above the horizonal line to a level of $4,261. This means that, compared with their average earnings before they got married, men's incomes increased after they married. The change in maritial status (single to married) is accompanied by a change in income (on average, an increase of about $4,000). It is important to remember that the men in this study married at different ages, some in their teens and others in their early thirties. The change in income associated with marriage is the *average* for all such men and may be somewhat larger or smaller at different ages. The next section discusses how incomes change as a result of the number of years a man remains married to his spouse and of other factors related to his age.

Figure 4.1 also indicates substantial differences associated with remarriage. Men's annual incomes are about $2,746 lower after they remarry than before. Such a finding accords with what one would predict. Remarriage is not the same as a first marriage because there are few, if any, normative guidelines associated with it. In many ways, remarriage resembles cohabitation. Both are common forms of relationships; both resemble marriage in certain ways; yet neither is as completely institutionalized in law, custom, or religion as marriage. Remarriages may be governed by the same laws as first marriages, but they are more complicated arrangements that are not as clearly defined by convention. What is a stepfather to be called by his wife's children? What is a stepfather's role in discipline? How are exspouses involved in holiday celebrations? In such small ways, remarriages must be created by each couple, with little guidance in the customs of our society. Remarriages are what Cherlin (1978) called "incomplete institutions."

There are no significant income consequences of divorce or widowerhood for men. In this and all similar figures, no bar is drawn when effects are statistically not significant. Fewer than half of 1% of the sample experienced widowerhood during the study period. The outcome studied here is annual income, rather

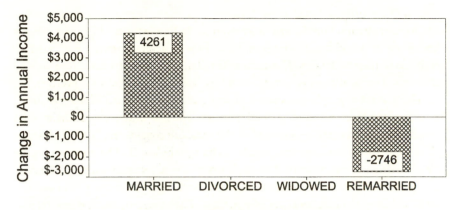

Change in Marital Status

Figure 4.1. *Average change in annual income as a result of changes in marital status.* Bars are shown only for statistically significant effects. Data from the National Longitudinal Survey of Youth: 1979–1993.

than standard of living. Divorced men may indeed experience a decline in their standard of living if their incomes are shared with a former spouse. However, there is no evidence that actual income declines for men as a result of a divorce. The results for first marriage and remarriages support the view that normative marriage is a factor that promotes achievements. Marriage increases income, and remarriage reduces it.

The second graph, Figure 4.2, presents the results for the number of weeks worked in the past year. Probably to a greater degree than is true for income, men have some control over the number of weeks worked. Some may be able to work longer hours at their place of employment. Others may take second jobs. And probably many factors would lead a man to reduce the number of weeks worked (e.g., health problems, child-care issues, or the need to care for other members of the family).

Once married, men work a little more than two more weeks per year (again, the effects of age have been controlled). However, following a divorce, men's work commitment declines by about a week per year. Remarriage has even greater consequences, reducing the number of weeks worked by about three per year. These effects may be treated as additive. That is, one can add the effects of divorce to those of remarriage to arrive at a rough estimate of the combined effects of these events. Doing so suggests that divorce and remarriage are costly transitions for men. As Figure 4.1 showed, remarriage brings about a reduction in income, and the reduced number of weeks worked may be part of the reason. In their transition from one marriage to another, men reduce their work commitments significantly (i.e., the effects of a divorce plus a remarriage are about four fewer weeks worked per year).

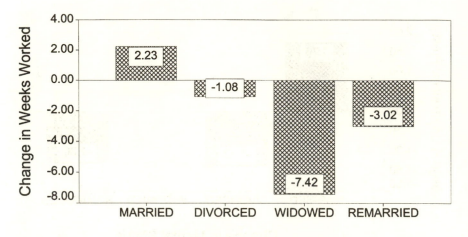

Change in Marital Status

Figure 4.2. *Average change in weeks worked as a result of changes in marital status.* Data from the National Longitudinal Survey of Youth: 1979–1993.

Finally, we consider the results for occupational level. Before presenting these findings, I offer a word about the way occupation is measured. Sociologists have asked large nationally representative samples of Americans to evaluate the overall social standing of occupations—that is, the prestige or honor accorded to people who typically occupy them. These studies have consistently found that Americans have a clear sense of where jobs stand in the hierarchy of prestige. Judges typically receive the highest scores and unskilled laborers the lowest. The scale used to represent jobs ranges over about 90 points. A 1-point difference represents the distinction between, for example, an architect (score = 85) and a college professor (score = 84), an elementary school teacher (score = 71) and a secondary school teacher (score = 70), or an electrician (score = 44) and a motion picture projectionist (score = 43). Occupational prestige is related to earnings, of course, though there are notable exceptions to this relationship. Some occupations rank highly in terms of prestige (e.g., clergy) yet garner relatively low salaries.

Figure 4.3 shows that marriage brings about an almost 2-point gain in occupational prestige. Divorce and remarriage, however, have the opposite effect. Such achievement effects of changes in marital status are particularly noteworthy because occupational prestige is a relatively stable trait of American workers. A particular man may enter and leave the workforce or increase or decrease the number of weeks worked. He is less likely, however, to change the kind of job he does. Judges, elementary school teachers, or electricians, for example, may earn more or less or work more or fewer weeks per year. But such men are less likely to enter different lines of work. Therefore, the findings about occupational prestige are remarkable, despite their relatively small magnitudes.

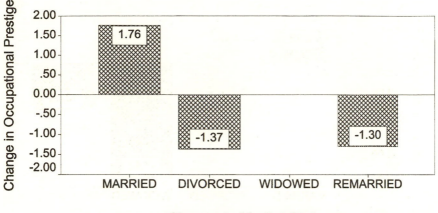

Change in Marital Status

Figure 4.3. *Average change in occupational prestige as a result of changes in marital status.* Bars are shown only for statistically significant effects. Data from the National Longitudinal Survey of Youth: 1979–1993.

Taken together, these results portray marriage as a positive force in men's adult achievements. They also reveal the negative consequences of ending a marriage or entering another. Such findings are a necessary first step in the search for the means by which they happen. If the argument of this work is valid, identifying aspects of marriage that help explain these results should be possible. In particular, the various dimensions of normative marriage should help explain the beneficial consequences of wedlock.

Yet American marriages differ in how closely they conform to each of the normative dimensions outlined earlier. For example, in some households, the husband is not the head. Some married couples remain childless. And the idea of monogamy is clearly a different concept among remarried than among continuously married individuals. The view of marriage as part of adult masculinity implies that the measures of achievement just reviewed would vary according to how marriages conform to or deviate from the normative model. As marriages change from more to less normative, there should be corresponding changes in men's achievements.

Married Men and Variations in Normative Marriage

Now we can shift attention from changes in marital status to changes in married men's lives. I have already established the fact that getting married improves men's attainment. The next task is to determine whether variations in their marriages have similar effects on achievement.

The dimensions of normative marriage must be measured. This assessment requires some preliminary discussion because there are no generally recognized measures of concepts like maturity, free choice, fidelity, or whether the husband is the head of the household. For each normative dimension of marriage, reasonable measures must be developed and then shown to be related to income, weeks worked, and occupational prestige. The six dimensions of normative marriage outlined in earlier chapters are (1) *free choice,* (2) *maturity,* (3) *heterosexuality,* (4) *husband as head of the household,* (5) *fidelity/monogamy,* and (6) *parenthood.*

Free Choice

Free choice refers to the fact that marriage is entered into freely on the basis of personal attraction and love. Because mate selection is a personal and free choice, desirability is central to the decision. Presumably, the decision to marry, or remain married, reflects evaluations of the costs and benefits of doing so (among other things). For this reason, marriage may be characterized as occurring in a market. People are more or less attractive (as potential or actual spouses) relative to others, and that attractiveness establishes a person's value in the marriage market.

Market processes do not end when people marry. In their married lives, spouses continue to evaluate their circumstances. If the costs of remaining married are significantly higher than the benefits of divorce, then a marriage will end. This simple observation is neatly summarized by sociologist Bernard Farber's (1964) description of modern American marriage patterns.

Farber noted that in traditional monogamous cultures, one enters the marriage market at maturity and exits at marriage. In societies with high divorce rates, however, one remains in the field of eligible spouses (in the marriage market) even after marriage. This latter pattern he called "permanent availability."

However, permanent availability does not mean that one remains equally attractive as a potential spouse. Indeed, regardless of age, income, or any other personal attribute, a man's position in the marriage market changes for reasons beyond his control. Most importantly, the number of unmarried women available as potential alternative spouses changes with time and age. Women tend to marry at somewhat younger ages than men. Moreover, men have higher death rates than women (age for age). And women have lower remarriage rates than men. As a result of such factors, the number of unmarried men and women of *roughly similar ages* in the population is rarely equal. Indeed, the relative number of unmarried men and women of similar ages studied in the NLSY changes markedly in the years of early adulthood. The marriage market for most men under 35 consists of unmarried women of roughly similar ages (within five years in either direction). As a result, there are changes each year in a man's "value" in that market. Of course, some men are able to marry women who are much younger (and some, in fact, marry women much older). However, most unmarried women will marry a man of very similar age—no more than two or three years older, on average. This is particularly true among people under the age of 35 (U.S. Bureau of the Census, 1996b: Table 14).

The age-specific sex ratio expresses the number of males of a particular age per 100 females that age. Such ratios calculated for unmarried people provide an indication of the number of unmarried women relative to unmarried men of comparable ages. If the ratio is 100, this means that roughly equal numbers of un-married men and women of a particular age are in the marriage market. If the ratio increases to 125, this means that there are 125 men for every 100 women.

Among those in their late teens to early twenties, the sex ratio is almost equal, with about 11 unmarried men for every 10 unmarried women (unmarried means divorced, widowed, or never married). By the time men are in their mid-to-late twenties, the ratio has climbed to about 13 men per 10 women. In the early thir-ties, the sex ratio begins to drop sharply due to differential mortality and remar-riage rates. And by the early forties, there are actually only 8 unmarried men for each 10 unmarried women (U.S. Bureau of the Census, 1994).

When there are more unmarried men than women, there is more competition for each woman than when the reverse is true. Alternatively, the costs of searching for a spouse are higher for men when the sex ratio is skewed (more unmarried men than women). Under such conditions, the benefits of remaining married are greater because the costs of leaving are higher. The higher the sex ratio, the more valuable a man's marriage is (relative to the alternatives). The higher the sex ratio, the *less valuable a man is* as a potential spouse in the larger marriage market. As the value of a man's marriage increases (and his value in the marriage market de-clines), there should be an increase in his achievements.

One can easily test this proposition by studying how married men's achieve-ments change as the age-specific sex ratio changes. For every combination of men's ages and calendar years, I have recorded the national sex ratio of unmarried men to women in five-year age groups. Thus, for example, in 1985, there is a different sex ratio for 20-year-old men than for 26-year-old men. And as each man ages, the prevailing sex ratio applicable to him also changes. The question is whether achieve-ment increases as the sex ratio increases (i.e., as men's marriages become more valuable relative to the alternatives).

Maturity

Marriage is associated with the assumption of adult responsibilities, emancipation from parents, termination of formal (legal) parental obligations, and indepen-dence from others. Married couples typically establish their own domicile and family economy. Thus, maturity and independence are closely related concepts, both associated with marriage. Although parents and others continue to be im-portant sources of help and assistance to married people, the customary assump-tion is that the married couple will become financially independent shortly after marriage. Most help received from parents is in the form of baby-sitting and services rather than income. Moreover, the financial support parents do provide is typically concentrated in the early years of marriage and declines with time. Normative marriage, therefore, is a financially independent union.

The typical American marriage today includes an employed husband and an employed wife. So the question is how much of a couple's total income is produced by both spouses—what proportion of their total income do they produce? In the event that earnings/salaries are not sufficient to meet the needs of the married couple, other sources of income may be used. For couples whose joint incomes fall below the official poverty threshold, for example, there are various types of federal and state assistance (e.g., food stamps, housing assistance, disability compensation). Gifts from others, such as parents, siblings, or friends, are another possible source of supplemental income.

To measure the level of financial independence of the married couple, I express their combined earnings (from jobs and self-employment) as a proportion of their total family income (including gifts, loans, transfer payments, and other forms of assistance). At one extreme, all family income is from sources other than the husband's and wife's labor force activities. At the other extreme, there is no additional family income beyond what one or both spouses produce. A married couple might be financially independent without *any* labor-force involvement if they earn large amounts of investment income. However, there is little evidence of significant amounts of such income in the NLSY. For that reason, earnings adequately capture each spouse's contribution to total family income.

Not only the newly married rely on sources of income other than their own. The average level of family self-sufficiency among all married men in this national sample is 85% (i.e., 85% of total family income is a result of wages and salaries). This figure varies from a low of 66% for those married less than a year to a high of 90% for those married fourteen years. In short, there is typically some amount of economic dependence among men under the age of 36 regardless of how long they have been married.

Because this proportion increases relative to the level of the married couple's independence of others' assistance, it is a direct measure of financial independence, or maturity (as that term is used here). The research question, therefore, is whether men's achievements increase as the family's independence increases.

Heterosexuality

The close association of marriage with presumptions about heterosexuality is part of the argument advanced in this book. Marriage is a public statement about object choice, and married men are not called upon to defend their sexual orientation. This may be one explanation for some of the results already presented. There is no way to measure this dimension of men's lives as it may change in marriage because so long as a man is married, he is ostensibly in a heterosexual relationship. Therefore, it is impossible to examine the importance of this dimension of normative marriage for men's achievements because it is a constant.

Husband as Head

American marriages are undoubtedly more egalitarian today than they were in the past. And as I showed in an earlier chapter, there is fairly broad support for the idea of equality in marriage. Legal and social changes have established the presumption of gender equality in marriage for most people. However, as also noted, acceptance of this ideal is not the same as accomplishing it. Women continue to do most of the routine housework, and men continue to earn the majority of the family income.

Income is central to any understanding of equality in marriage. No matter how dedicated two married people are to the principle of equal status in the family, that commitment will be more difficult if the two earn very different incomes. Many other facets of a marriage are secondary to income. For example, a common dilemma many married couples face is whether to move to a distant location for the sake of accepting a promotion offered to one spouse. Doing so typically means that the other partner must quit a job. What, if any, predictions might we make about how couples will resolve this dilemma? One is obvious. It is more likely that such a couple will decide to move if the higher-earning spouse's income will increase (i.e., it is unlikely that the higher-earning spouse will quit a job).

Even though husbands and wives might be judged equal or unequal on many dimensions of family life, income will have the greater consequence and be accorded the most importance.

To evaluate the equality of spouses' incomes, I calculate a measure that expresses the difference between earnings of the two married persons as a proportion of their combined earnings. I subtract the wife's earnings from the husband's and divide this difference by the combined earnings of both. If the wife is responsible for all earnings, the result is -1.0. If the husband earns all the couple's earnings, the result is +1.0. If both have equal earnings, the result is 0.0. As this measure increases from zero, it indexes greater inequality (see Brines, 1993) and indicates that the husband earns more than his wife.

In the course of a marriage, this measure is likely to shift many times. Upward changes likely result from one or two possibilities. First, a husband's earnings may increase while his wife's do not. Or a wife's earnings may decline while her husband's do not. Either would produce an increase in the husband's relative earnings. In modern marriages, however, a wife likely enters or re-enters the labor force (e.g., after leaving to have a child). Such shifts would reduce the husband's relative earnings. In short, changes in the husband's earnings are *not* the only way by which this measure might change.

The research question is whether increases in a husband's relative earnings are associated with increases in his achievements.

Fidelity and Monogamy

These related concepts refer to the exclusivity of marriage partners. It would be desirable to know whether spouses are faithful in their marriages, but this cannot be determined with any confidence without carefully designed studies focused on this issue (e.g., Laumann et al., 1995).

Monogamy, however, *is* a related and measurable idea. Monogamy implies that a marriage should endure. Our marriage ceremonies typically ask that we pledge ourselves until death. And even though many marriages do not survive so long, the longer they continue, the *more* monogamous we might think of them. In the first few years of marriages begun in the last two decades, the certainty that one's wife is reliably and dependably one's spouse forever is surely tempered by the realization that many marriages end in divorce. With time, however, the certainty that a marriage will endure increases. As couples negotiate the vagaries of married life together, some will resolve the problems and others will not. Those who are able to hold their marriage together come to share a certainty that the marriage *will* endure, despite future challenges. For this reason, I will measure monogamy as the simple count of years of marriage to one spouse. The research question is whether men's achievements increase as a marriage continues.

The measure of years in a particular marriage is reset to zero for those who remarry. Therefore, two men who have been married 10 out of the past 15 years may have very different scores for this measure in a particular year if one has remarried and the other has not.

Parenthood

Most married couples have children rather early in their marriages. Indeed, most have more than one child. The critical transition is that associated with the birth of the first child. Subsequent births may add responsibilities (e.g., additional child-care tasks), but the difference between a childless couple and one with one child is clearly greater than that between parents of one and two children.

The research question is whether becoming a parent is associated with an increase in a man's achievements. To deal with the possibility that additional children have effects beyond those associated with the initial transition to fatherhood, I also record information on any additional children added to the family who are offspring of the husband.

The transition to becoming a father happens, for purposes of this research, *only* when the child is the husband's legal offspring (born to his wife, or adopted). Therefore, a man who marries a woman who has custody of one or more children is not treated as having become a "father" for purposes of this research because stepchildren do not carry the same implications for men as biological or adopted children do. Parenthood matters in this research because *custody of children* is one of the most enduring of adult obligations. Once assumed, parental responsibilities may not be easily abandoned. Even though stepfathers may be very effective parents, their obligations are based on affection and are not bound by formal custody considerations.

I have outlined the basic research questions designed to show whether variations in normative marriage are associated with variations in men's achievements. If they are, we become more confident about the basic idea that marriage is a form of masculine identity and expression for men. I turn now to the results of the analyses.

The Effects of Normative Marriage on Men's Achievements

To make the presentation of results easier, I rely on graphs based on multivariate equations found in Appendix A. Each of the dimensions of normative marriage is measured as discussed above. In these graphs, I show how each dimension affects achievement by charting their effects from the minimum to the maximum amount of change. That is, I show how changes in each dimension would affect the outcome when such changes are the minimum value (least normative) and the maximum value (most normative). This strategy makes it possible to gauge the maximum possible consequence of each dimension, even though few men would experience changes across the entire range of the dimension. Few men, in other words, progress from earning none of the family income to earning all of it (i.e., the full range of the measure for maturity or economic independence). The line drawn for this and the other dimensions of marriage, therefore, should be viewed as an indication of how much a man's life *could* change as a result of that dimension of his marriage.

Income

Men's annual incomes change in response to changes in the degree to which their marriage conforms to the normative model. In fact, every measure of normative marriage is found to produce effects consistent with those predicted.

Consider first the measure of free choice or market value (i.e., age-specific sex ratio). The plotted results in Figure 4.4 show that a change over the entire range of this factor would be associated with a $3,169 increase in annual income. Few men, as noted, would experience this large a change. Nonetheless, the large effect is consistent with the idea that men's incomes rise as their value outside their marriages declines. Alternatively, men's incomes rise as the value of their marriage increases.

The measure of maturity (family economic independence) also produces very

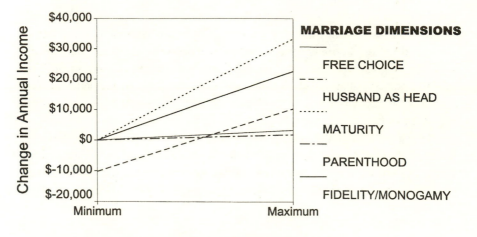

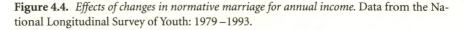

Change from Minimum to Maximum

Figure 4.4. *Effects of changes in normative marriage for annual income.* Data from the National Longitudinal Survey of Youth: 1979–1993.

large effects. The consequence of changing from complete dependence on others for family income to complete independence (the maximum possible difference) is an increase of about $33,000 in a man's income.

One might argue that the effects go in the opposite direction, that increases in a man's income bring about an increase in the family's independence. This is surely a possibility to consider. However, the longitudinal nature of the study gives some assurance that the effects move as postulated. Since it is possible to study men over time, it is possible to determine the order of marital events. When the methods capture these effects, therefore, there is good reason to believe that independence fosters greater income.

However, perhaps both income and family independence change simultaneously. Indeed, with no other change in the family (i.e., change in the wife's income or in contributions from other sources), independence is certain to rise as men's incomes increase. Because the measure of family independence is computed by adding the husband's and wife's earnings (before dividing by the total family income), there is an inherent relationship between the two measures. But changes in men's earnings are only *one* way in which the measure of family independence changes.

A man's family also becomes more independent when his wife's income increases. And it becomes more independent when outside sources of income decrease. The total family income, by which the sum of husband's and wife's earnings is divided, is *not* necessarily the sum of the spouse's earnings. Rather, it is the total income reported by the family from *all* sources, including transfer payments, gifts, loans, and payments from government programs. For this reason, family independence may vary due to changes in the husband's earnings, the wife's earnings, or other sources of family income. Each of these possibilities occurs in the lives of men studied for this research. Moreover, the relationship between men's earnings and family independence is not much greater than that between the wife's earnings and family independence (correlations of .45 and .39, respectively). These results, and the longitudinal nature of the data, lend support to the view that changes in family independence foster changes in men's earnings. However, given the reservations noted, conclusions about this dimension of normative marriage must be withheld until other types of adult achievement have been considered in the following sections.

There is also a strong effect for the measure of husband's relative earnings (i.e., "husband as head"). Were the family finances to change from complete dependence on the wife (all income in the family earned by the wife) to the opposite extreme (all income in the family earned by the husband), the average change in the man's earnings would be about $20,000 (i.e., a drop of -$10,222 under conditions of complete dependence and an increase of +$10,222 under conditions of complete independence).

The simplest interpretation of these results is that a man responds to declines in his wife's earnings by increasing his own earnings. Less likely, but also possible, men respond to increases in wives' earnings by reductions in their own. The most important factor in determining the relative earnings of husbands and wives is the *wife's* earnings. Changes in wives' earnings are more closely related to the relative income of the spouses than are changes in husbands' earnings. The correlations between (changes in) husband's and wife's earnings and the measure of relative earnings are .08 (husband) and -.37 (wife). Not surprisingly, women's earnings are more variable over time. Men, it appears, respond to such variations as predicted.

The effect for the measure of fidelity/monogamy reveals the anticipated results. As a marriage continues, men's incomes increase by about $1,826 per year. For men continuously married for 10 years, for example, this means an average increase of $18,260. As with all other effects described, the consequence of celebrating additional wedding anniversaries is the *net* of age and all other dimensions. Thus, one may say that *in addition* to any changes associated with relative income, or family independence, the simple duration of a marriage contributes to men's incomes.

Finally, when men become fathers in their marriages, annual income rises by about $1,705. Moreover, there are no additional consequences, either positive or negative, for subsequent children related to income.

In short, for every dimension of normative marriage measured in this research, large effects in the expected direction were found. Normative marriage appears to be associated with higher earnings for husbands. Before taking such findings as strong evidence to support the basic arguments about the meaning of marriage in men's lives, however, we must consider the other indicators of adult achievement to see if they reflect similar trends.

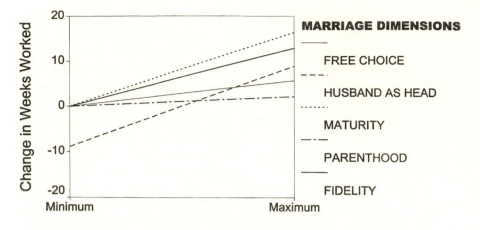

Change from Minimum to Maximum

Figure 4.5. *Effects of changes in normative marriage for annual weeks worked.* Data from the National Longitudinal Survey of Youth: 1979–1993.

Weeks Worked

The results for work commitment do, in fact, add strong support to the findings already presented. Every dimension of normative marriage affects this outcome in the direction expected. As noted earlier, a man's work commitment is probably more under his control than his income is. For men who are paid hourly wages, the two are obviously related. For men who are paid salaries, however, the connection is less direct. In some jobs, weeks missed do not necessarily translate into lost earnings, just as additional weeks worked do not necessarily translate into additional earnings. As a result, the results for weeks worked are somewhat stronger than those found for income.

Figure 4.5 shows how the various dimensions of normative marriage are related to the number of weeks worked in the past calendar year. Men appear to respond to their changing value in the marriage market by increasing their work commitment. Over the course of 15 years, changes in the sex ratio for any *particular man* are about three-quarters as large as the maximum effect plotted in the graph. Over the course of that many years, declines in a man's value on the marriage market produce an increase of three or four more weeks worked per year.

Does this mean that men actually calculate their value in the marriage market and respond by working more? Perhaps some men do. But marriage is not likely experienced as the set of discrete dimensions analyzed here. Rather, the findings attributed to the various dimensions of marriage should be seen as elements that combine to produce a coherent model for men. As they age, and as their marriages endure, the model changes. Patterns for dealing with the routine and exceptional events in life emerge. Men and women adjust their schedules to one another. The arrival of children brings about a change in the model, as does the aging of parents. Geographic moves require shifts in schedules and patterns. In these and countless other ways, men (and women) change in their marriages. They change for many reasons, only some of which are recognized and acknowledged. Changes in work patterns associated with changes in the sex ratio, therefore, do not mean that men consciously recognize their value on the marriage market. But somehow that value translates into different work patterns. Some men may work more to be able to afford a larger house, a new car, dance lessons for a child, or other amenities. Some men may work more for the sake of advancing their careers. This fact remains: as the value of a man's marriage increases (i.e., his value in the marriage market declines), his work effort increases too.

Large effects are also associated with the measure of family independence (maturity). Husbands in families that do not depend on any other sources of income (i.e., other than that generated by the married partners) work more weeks per year than husbands in families highly dependent on others. Were a family to traverse the entire range of economic independence (from complete dependence to complete independence) the corresponding increase in the husband's work effort would encompass about 16 weeks per year.

Before we too quickly assume that strong connections exist between variations in the number of weeks men work and variations in their incomes, we should note that these two are actually very *weakly* related. The correlation between changes in weeks worked and changes in income is almost zero ($r = .08$), while that between actual weeks worked (not changes in weeks worked) and actual income is only minimally stronger ($r = .11$). Therefore, it cannot be said that the increases shown for income in the last section are the *result* of increases in work effort. Indeed, given the weak relationship between the two, it is striking how similarly changes in marriage affect both income and weeks worked.

Much the same can be said about relative earnings (the measure of husband as head of the family). As the figure shows, were a situation to change from complete dependence on the wife to the extreme opposite, there would be a corresponding change in the husband's work effort of almost 18 weeks. More interesting, however, men whose incomes (for whatever reasons) drop below that of their wives actually work fewer weeks per year.

As was true for income, these results speak directly to the centrality of the normative belief that husbands are the principal wage earners in a family. These findings show that as men come to occupy such a traditional (and normative) role in their marriages, their work efforts and incomes rise. Family authority or power, at least to the extent that such things are associated with relative income, appear to be a stimulus in men's married lives. As a man's position as head of the family is more and more firmly established, he responds by working and earning more—presumably further confirming that position.

For the measure of fidelity and monogamy, recall that years married to one particular spouse is a measure used to reflect our belief that the presumption of permanence (i.e., monogamy) grows with every passing year. Indeed, the results show a large increase in weeks worked as a marriage continues. Once all the other dimensions discussed above have been considered (i.e., their effects removed), each additional year married to a particular spouse is associated with an increase of about four days' work per year (.90 of a week = 4.5 days).

Every man in this study is between 14 and 36 years old, so all the results must be tempered by the possibility that things change in the early years of marriage in ways they may not in later years. The average number of years married for these men is about 4 (3.8), even though some have been married 14 of the 15 years of the research. For that reason, it probably does not make sense to assert that 10 additional years of marriage leads to 9 additional weeks worked (i.e., .90 × 10 = 9 weeks). To know how the continuing marriage might affect men later in life, we would need to revisit this group of men in another 10 years. Until we are able to do that, we can say only that the persistence of a marriage leads to greater work efforts in the first 5 or 10 years, at least.

The transition to parenthood has modest effects on men's labor-force commitments. On average, the arrival of the first child is associated with a little more than two additional weeks worked. Although modest, such an effect is noteworthy for the direction of effects. One might imagine that a new father would actually work fewer hours in order to participate in the newly created child-care tasks for his family. Indeed, men are involved in child care, as other researchers have shown. However, that involvement does not jeopardize their work. Rather, work appears to assume even greater importance to men once they become married fathers. Additional children do not appear to add consequences for men's work efforts.

The effort represented by the number of weeks worked varies as marriages change and endure. Men appear to respond to their wives' earnings and the family's economic dependence on others. They also respond to becoming parents. And, last, men respond to their changing market value outside of their marriage. I turn finally to the measure of occupational prestige, arguably the most stable of the three measures of adult achievement.

Occupational Prestige

Marriage has much the same consequence for men's occupational success as it does for their incomes and work effort. The results summarized in Figure 4.6 show that, with but one exception, every dimension of marriage has the predicted consequences.

As the value of men's marriages increases (i.e., their value in the marriage market declines), their occupational achievements increase too, albeit minimally. Still, given that each effect plotted in these graphs is completely independent (ef-

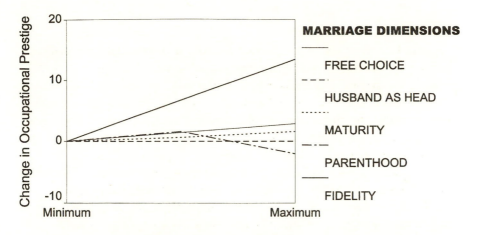

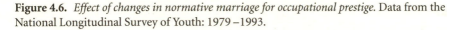

Change from Minimum to Maximum

Figure 4.6. *Effect of changes in normative marriage for occupational prestige.* Data from the National Longitudinal Survey of Youth: 1979 –1993.

fects due to one dimension are unrelated to those attributed to others), the consequence of this one dimension is notable. Changes in this single dimension are associated with increases of almost three points in occupational prestige.

Likewise, family independence (maturity) is associated with small but positive changes in occupational prestige—about one point at most. Just as all preceding figures have shown, the stability of a man's marriage (fidelity/monogamy) has very strong positive consequences. Men's occupational prestige increases by almost an entire point with each wedding anniversary. Finally, becoming a parent appears to stimulate minor improvements in men's occupations (about 1.6 points). Additional children, however, do not continue to improve a man's occupational prestige. Rather, at a certain point, the beneficial consequences of becoming a father are lessened by additional children. The results show that each additional child (after the first) is associated with a small reduction in prestige (about half a point). Therefore, for men who have four or more children, the consequences of fatherhood are negligible. This determination is made by adding the effects of becoming a father (+1.6) to the negative effects of having three additional children (−1.5). For men who have more than four children, however, there is a slight negative consequence (e.g., +1.6 − 2.0 = −0.4).

Taken together, the results for occupational prestige largely mirror those for the other indicators of men's adult achievement. The effects are smaller, yet consistent in direction.

Conclusion

I began this investigation of the effects of marriage on men's achievements by considering the consequences of *changes* produced by marriage, divorce, or remarriage. At this stage of the research, the questions were elementary. Do transitions into and out of marriage lead to measurable changes in annual incomes, weeks worked, and occupational prestige? The answer is yes. Although varying in magnitude, the effects of getting married are consistently positive. Once married, men earn more, work more, and have better jobs.

The effects of marriage do not end, however, with the transition *into* matrimony. I also found that divorce had some negative consequences for men. A divorce reduces men's labor force commitment and occupational prestige, even though not significantly affecting income. However, remarriage had even more pronounced negative consequences. Men who remarry work less, earn less, and have less prestigious occupations than they did before their remarriages.

Unlike first marriages suffused with normative expectations, each remarriage must be negotiated anew. When a man first marries, he knows what is expected of him even if such expectations are the source of trouble in his marriage. Our cultural (normative) definition of marriage provides a template for the newly married husband. That template may, in fact, cause tension or even divorce. A man who assumes that he should be the head of the household may discover that his wife has very different ideas about marriage. A man who assumes that he should become a father may also discover that his desires are not shared. Regardless of how the normative dimensions of marriage are experienced in any first marriage, they provide a model if one is needed. But what is the model of a remarriage? Individual men may decide that their remarriage should differ from the first marriage in those elements that appear to have failed. But this is an individual decision—a reaction to the first marriage. Each man will face the task of defining a remarriage.

The problems of constructing a relationship in the absence of a normative definition are clearly reflected in the results presented in this chapter. And they help make the central point of my argument. The institutional aspect of marriage—the normative definition of it—distinguishes it from all other relationships. No union of two people is so well-defined, understood, and regulated as normative marriage. It is understandable, therefore, that marriage has *positive* consequences although remarriage has the opposite effects.

Having established the most basic relationships between transitions into and out of marriage and adult achievements, I turned to an examination of married men. The purpose was to consider *how* marriage produces its apparent effects and to emphasize the strength of the underlying argument of *Marriage in Men's Lives*. If the argument of this book is right, then it should be possible to show that variations in how closely a man's marriage conforms to the model of normative mar-

riage are related to variations in his adult achievements. The results were consistently supportive. The more closely a man's marriage conforms to the normative
model, the greater are his adult achievements. Moreover, shifts toward more normative marriages (declines in wives' relative earnings, more children, greater family economic independence, and a more competitive marriage market) lead to significantly higher levels of adult achievement.

At this point it is possible to make this assertion: normative marriage is good
for men's adult achievements. On a range of measures, and from a variety of ap-
proaches, the results of the analysis converge at this simple point.

NOTES

1. The research used pooled cross-section time-series with fixed effects methods. Each
year of information becomes a case (unit of analysis) for analysis. A single man interviewed
every year from 1979 through 1993 would contribute 15 person years. Each variable is represented as a deviation from the average for the particular man. For example, income in
1979 is expressed as a deviation from the average income for all years for this particular
man. The technique analyzes whether deviations on one variable (e.g., income) are greater
(or less) in the presence of marriage (also expressed as a deviation from the average of all
dummy variables for married/not married) than in the absence of marriage once the
changes associated with chronological age are removed. The resulting coefficients indicate
how much a variable changes, on average, when a man marries, independent of changes associated with age. Standard errors of regression coefficients have been adjusted to compensate for the consequences of pooling. The error coefficient from OLS is multiplied by the
ratio of

$$\frac{\sqrt{(NT - K)}}{\sqrt{(NT - N - T - K - 1)}}$$

where $T = 15$ waves, $N =$ sample size for the equation, $K =$ number of independent
variables. In fixed effects analysis, regression is forced through the origin. All equations are restricted to men with annual incomes of less than $1,000,000.

2. There is a possibility that the effect of marriage differs according to certain such
factors, of course. For example, the average change in income following marriage may be
larger for black men than white men. Such interaction effects were not part of the analysis
presented, although they were studied in preliminary analyses.

◆ 5 ◆

Personal Communities

The personal connections that link individuals define our society and integrate each of us into a social world made up of networks of others. We are likely known by the company we keep; certainly that is how we come to know ourselves. In others' reflected appraisal we see ourselves.

Every relationship, no matter how fleeting, is a mirror in which we see the impressions we make. The attractive, intelligent, trustworthy, or faithful person enjoys such reputations only because they are forged in contact with other people. Likewise, the miserly scoundrel is known as such because he acted improperly in his dealings with others. The fabric of personal identity—including notions of gender—is woven into relationships. So we may speak of the institution of marriage (or politics or the economy), knowing that such institutions are abstractions that describe patterns of relationships. At the personal level of day-to-day life, individuals experience every institution as a series of actual connections. Each of us experiences the world most forcefully as a number of communities, some actually geographic, but most comprised of loose connections among individuals who share something in common.

Such networks, or *personal communities* (Fischer, 1982), are chiefly the result of individual choices. Even if we have little control over our relatives, we have some discretion in how much time to spend with them. Each day we make minor decisions about whether and when to see others, whether to help, and whether to seek help. These choices and decisions, however, are not completely free. Almost everyone recognizes constraints. Maintaining cordial relations with one's co-workers, for example, is a part of most jobs. But close romantic relationships between subordinates and superiors in the workplace may be prohibited by formal or informal policies. Relationships with relatives, likewise, are fashioned in response to widely held ideas about what is right and proper. The same may be said about contacts at church, in the neighborhood, or in school. So, on the one hand, we construct our personal communities deliberately (even if casually) as we decide that this person but not that person will be included, or that this relationship but not that one will be maintained. On the other hand, our decisions and choices in such matters are influenced by social convention and custom.

Even though we have choice in forging connections with others, the circumstances of our lives impose obvious limitations. Personal communities are built in particular times and places. A rich man will encounter others whom those of more modest means will never meet. A young man who enlists in the armed forces will meet people whom his civilian siblings will not. Parents of young children will meet other parents they would not have met had they remained childless. Residents of small rural areas will have fewer contacts than residents of large metropolitan regions. And those who work the night shift will have different choices in their personal communities than those who work conventional nine-to-five schedules. In each of these and countless other ways, the organization of society structures personal communities. Work, social class, religion, school, and kinship are powerful forces that affect our choices of friends and associates.

What is the role of marriage in the organization of personal relationships? Like other circumstances, marriage is both a limitation and an opportunity for the creation and maintenance of relationships. This chapter demonstrates how men's social lives change when they marry. It will also show how normative marriage influences the personal communities of married men.

Marriage and Personal Communities

Why would men's personal relationships be altered by their marriages? To begin, very obvious and ordinary changes might alter a new groom's social life. Marriage may mean a relocation in residence. It certainly means that activities will need to be coordinated with a partner. The demands on time are different for single and married people. Marriage requires a great deal of scheduling to coordinate the work hours of two spouses and, possibly, that of children's schools. Research has shown, for example, that married couples stagger their working hours (i.e., work different hours) to accommodate the peculiar schedule of most primary schools. This makes it possible for one spouse to be home before and after school hours, but it also reduces the amount of time couples have together (Kingston and Nock, 1985; Nock and Kingston, 1987). Certain problems of coordination are well-known issues in marriage. Changing jobs, going back to school, or accepting promotions all mean a realignment of lives. Even having dinner together or going to a movie may require some planning. In such large and small ways, the use of time is altered by marriage, with significant cumulative consequences. Married men allocate their available time differently than they did before marrying. And this has implications for personal communities.

Berk described the married couple's household as a *gender factory* (1985) because in the routine aspects of married life men and women develop and experience their gender roles. As husbands or wives, married people create an individual and a shared life that includes friends, associates, relatives, and various groups and organizations. In constructing such networks, husbands and wives *display* their masculinity or femininity by making decisions about whom they will associate with and what sorts of activities they will pursue. As noted earlier, gender displays are much more than superficial appearances. The way men and women act *as* men or women (i.e., how they appear to others) has very clear implications for how they view themselves. As we saw earlier, gender tends to coalesce across its various dimensions (i.e., presentation of self, gender identity, object choice). So the man who seems masculine by virtue of his actions and appearance probably thinks of himself that way, as well. If marriage is a framework for masculinity, then it affects men's personal communities and relationships with others in predictable ways.

For example, married men do less housework than they did before they married. Although probably a commonplace observation among many newly married couples, this is actually a very telling observation. Why would a man who cooked and cleaned for himself do less of these things once he is married? There are several obvious possibilities. For one, marriage may bring about some economy of scale. The man who did his own cooking may now share that task with his wife. Each spouse, thereby, reduces (by some amount) the effort once committed to this household task. Alternatively, there may be absolutely less that needs to be done. The married man may have certain labor-saving conveniences that he didn't have when he was single—a microwave oven, washing machine, or dryer, for example. The reduction in housework following marriage may reflect a reduced need for it.

Some have argued that the customary gender-based division of tasks in married couples' households reflects rational economic decision making. Because men typically command higher salaries than women in the labor force, time spent on housework has greater costs for husbands. The rational household will allocate labor to minimize the economic consequences (Becker, 1981). If a husband's earnings exceed his wife's, a gender-based division of labor is economically rational. For such a strategy to work, of course, hours in one task (e.g., cleaning the house) must be exchangeable for more profitable hours in another (e.g., working at paid employment).

Another possibility focuses on how marriage informs a sense of adult masculinity. Some types of housework are culturally defined as *women's*. This is particularly true of tasks performed exclusively in the dwelling: cleaning, ironing, or cooking, for example. If a man accepts this premise, there will be some tension about doing those tasks. Moreover, if he thinks *others in his personal community* accept it, there will be even more tension over doing housework. A man might overcome his own personal prejudices about doing the cleaning but will have more difficulty overcoming his perception that others who matter in his life might think him deviant.

The remarkable thing about housework is that the norms pertaining to it seem to *inhere* in the institution of marriage. Cleaning, laundry, or other routine daily household maintenance tasks do not appear to carry gender implications so long as there is no other person around who might do them. But once a man is married, there *is* another person. Research has shown repeatedly that indoor household tasks are performed primarily by wives — even when both spouses have similar employment (Shelton, 1992; Thompson, 1993).

The example of housework illustrates how marriage and routine activities are related by virtue of the gendered nature of both. Housework, per se, is not a form of association. However, directly or indirectly, it probably has implications for personal contacts with others. Housework is the core around which other activities revolve. It structures life in obvious and subtle ways, both tangible and symbolic. Decisions about who does what involve other choices about whose job matters most, whose time is more valuable, who has more power in the family, and who is more competent in various endeavors. Beyond the prosaic consequences of housework for time and energy available, such tasks carry strong implications for notions of gender identity. Now, let us expand our consideration of the consequences of marriage in men's lives by considering various types of relationships, beginning with relationships with relatives.

Relationships with Kin

The central universal dimensions of adult masculinity discussed in earlier chapters involved provision of needs and protection (of home and family) and married fatherhood. Husbands must, therefore, attend to the needs of their families. Men become relatives of many more people once they are married. A wife's parents, her siblings, or her children from a previous marriage are all *close* kin by common standards. Although a man's primary obligation must be to his wife and children, he must also be sensitive to his role as needs provider and protector of the larger kinship including his parents, his wife's parents, and possibly others. To neglect a parent, or a wife's mother or father, for example, is unacceptable behavior for a husband. Indeed, marriage creates extensive obligations among men and their kin (as it also does for women) — obligations that were nonexistent or much weaker before marriage (Rossi and Rossi, 1990). Marriage establishes several individuals for whom husbands may be held responsible — all kin to varying degrees.

Socializing with relatives is often done as a couple. Therefore, men may see more of their kin because their wives arrange the visits. Even without any sense of kinship obligation, therefore, it is likely that, once married, men will be more closely involved in the lives of relatives than before they married.

At the same time, counter-tendencies pull men away from home, family, and kin. The model of masculinity (forged in opposition to femininity) implies that gender identity for men is expressed as the antithesis of close, expressive, personal, and passive relationships. It calls for a life governed by rules and standards, wherein the man is responsible, not dependent, a world in which he is active, not passive. In their construction of personal communities, married men tend to develop relationships governed by rules rather than informal give-and-take. In other words, husbands favor relationships that do not require extensive work to establish and maintain. Rather, married men tend to pursue networks and contacts for which clearly established norms and rules exist. Many such contacts will not be kin. But involvement with relatives—influenced by custom and convention—is part of most marriages. For example, once a man marries, his relationship with his wife's mother and other in-laws is defined by various expectations and obligations.

The normative content of these relationships with relatives is easily illustrated. A man has less discretion in his relationships with in-laws than he does with neighbors or co-workers. There are certain things he is expected to do and certain ways he is expected to act as a son-in-law. He should visit on a regular basis. He is expected to remember birthdays and other special events, to send cards or gifts as appropriate. He may not do or act accordingly, but he may pay a price. A man may avoid all contact with in-laws and may actually be hostile toward them. However, that behavior will probably be seen as a violation of a shared sense of family morality. The fact that we recognize these limitations and expectations for in-law relationships means that we share and understand the rules governing them. Seen this way, relations with relatives are normative. Married men are expected to become involved in networks of kinship, to celebrate birthdays, holidays, and anniversaries with kin. Marriage should increase men's involvement in such networks.

Involvement in Religious Congregations

Other normatively patterned relationships are found in religious organizations. Not only are relationships with others in the church structured by rules and principles, they are also public. Private relationships include heavy doses of expressive sentiment, whereas public relationships are more likely to be imbued with restraint concerning personal matters, with greater emphasis placed on adequate performance. As a member of a congregation, a member of the choir, the leader of a Sunday school class, or member of the lay leadership, a man is known for how well he fulfills his obligations and responsibilities.

The type of relationships people have with other members of their synagogue or church often differ from those in secular settings. Indeed, this is one important reason for joining a congregation. It is the structured nature of ties among members that is the hallmark of congregation membership. All are bound together by their membership in a shared system of beliefs and customs. Repeated national surveys have shown that most Americans have a clear sense of what they want from their churches and synagogues. These studies show that the church is typically viewed as a locale for the expression of beliefs among those with common values: "They tend to view their churches less as sources of faith than as resources for their personal and family religious and spiritual needs" (Gallup and Castelli, 1989: 90). Nine in 10 Americans say they want religious training for their children, and 7 in 10 actually provide such education (1989: 66). There is something about the types of contacts one makes at church that distinguishes them from others. Church is something parents want for their children, and something most Americans want for themselves (85% of Americans attend religious services at least several times a year; one in four attends every week; 1989: 33). This book is not the place to consider the content of religious experiences. However, one very obvious aspect matters for our purposes. Churches are *organizations* no less than corporations, hospitals, or colleges. They have a structure and system of rules governing positions, authority, finances, and membership. They are so bureaucratic, in fact, that a majority of Americans (59%) complain that their churches and synagogues are too concerned with organizational issues at the expense of spiritual matters (1989: 88).

No matter what else people may get from their involvement in a congregation, members become participants in an organization. By their membership they agree to accept certain standards of behavior and to bind themselves to conformity with established organizational principles, as members of any organized group do.

Other Relationships: Co-workers and Friends

Although relatives and religious congregations provide important components of a personal community, they hardly exhaust the range of possibilities. I began with these two because they are the most clearly patterned relationships. Less textured, but still somewhat structured, are relationships with co-workers. Among co-workers, shared work experiences and well-established reputations in an organization will color most social contacts (i.e., each person will know the other by his or her position and reputation in the organization). Even on social occasions, co-workers are likely to dwell on matters of common concern at work. They are likely to regard one another as members of the organization. Each person's position in it will be part of his or her personal identity. The organization of work is an element of any such relationship and it will probably influence the nature of the contacts among co-workers. But the influence of this common membership is probably less significant than the influence of religion or kinship.

Relationships not clearly governed by strong normative principles are commonly known as *friendships*. A friend is someone with whom one lets down his hair, relaxes his guard, and acts like *himself*—that is, not as he is expected to act by others. When we act like ourselves, we eschew normative convention in favor of our own standards. Some types of organizations (e.g., hobby clubs) and individuals (e.g., old schoolmates) fall into this category of possible personal community members. Likewise, casual contacts with neighbors or those formed on evenings at bars or taverns are quite informal. All such relationships would be expected to decline with marriage, as emphasis is placed on rule-based associations.

Information about Personal Communities

To investigate how marriage alters men's personal networks and involvements with others, I rely on a large national study conducted in 1987–88 and again in 1992–94. The National Survey of Families and Households (NSFH) is a nationally representative study designed to assemble information on family life, marriage, cohabitation, and numerous related topics. In 1987, 2-hour personal interviews were conducted with 13,008 individuals over the age of 19 living in noninstitutional arrangements. In households with a married couple, one spouse provided the majority of the information about the household and children in it, but parallel interviews were conducted with the other partner. Approximately five years later, these same individuals were interviewed once again with a very similar questionnaire. In addition to the type of information gathered in 1987–88, the 1993 study included detailed histories of intimate relationships. These make it possible to know whether any marital transitions occurred between waves and, if so, what types.

Not all individuals interviewed in 1987 were located five or six years later. As a result, complete information (i.e., both time periods) exists for 10,008 of the original 13,008 members of the study. Since the interest of this project is men only, the results in this chapter are based on information from the 3,877 males who participated in both waves of the study. Finally, it was necessary to restrict the study to those of working age, for retirement brings about dramatic changes in household organization, social participation, and income that make it impossible to compare retired individuals with those still actively involved in the labor force. I limit this research to men who are no more than 64 years old. This leaves 3,277 adult men for whom sufficient information exists to answer the primary questions of this chapter. This is a large and nationally representative group of males that provides excellent assurances that factors such as geographic region or size of place do not confound the results.[1]

In the last chapter, it was possible to determine the consequences of marriage in the year immediately following the union because interviews were conducted annually. For this and the following chapter, information originates from two time points separated by five years. When the focus is on the consequences of various marital transitions (marriage, divorce, remarriage, widowerhood) therefore, we may be studying change over a period of time longer than one year. Some men in the NSFH experienced a marital transition five years ago, others only one year ago. This is not a problem so long as it is recognized that the reported consequences are average results following a marital transition at some point in the past five years.[2]

Measuring Social Participation and Personal Communities

The research in this chapter measures the effects of marriage on men's involvement with other people. But it is clearly impossible to study every single relationship with others. Therefore, several *types* of networks and relationships are examined. The goal is to identify a sufficient number of such connections to discern common trends and patterns, yet few enough to permit analysis. The primary concern is to identify relationships that are or are not governed by strong normative rules. In addition, it is important to include relationships with individuals as well as memberships in organizations as both types of affiliations define a man's personal community.

The NSFH includes information about relationships in several ways. All men were asked a series of questions about how often they got together socially with different categories of people. In addition, each man reported his participation in different organizations. The types of contacts studied in this chapter are listed here (from the most to the least structured by social norms):

1. *With relatives*
   Get together socially with relatives
2. *With religious congregations*
   Attend religious services at your church or synagogue
   Attend a social event at your church or synagogue
   Participate in church-affiliated groups (not including religious services)
3. *With co-workers or those in similar lines of employment*
   Get together socially with people you work with
   Participate in work-related groups, such as unions, farm organizations, or professional societies
4. *With loosely organized groups*
   Participate in sports, hobby or garden organizations, or discussion groups
   Participate in a group recreational activity such as bowling, golf, square dancing, etc.
   Participate in service clubs, fraternal groups, or political groups
5. *With neighbors and friends or associates*
   Get together socially with a neighbor
   Get together socially with friends who live outside your neighborhood
   Go to a bar or tavern [3]

When questions about getting together socially or attending church-related functions are considered, the issue is how many times, per year, men do each. For organizational membership, the focus is on active membership (participation or not in the past year).

The measures already mentioned differ in the type of contact considered. Some refer to individuals, others to organizations. In addition, some refer to very unstructured relationships not governed by rules (e.g., visiting friends, going to a bar or tavern), whereas others refer to somewhat more structured activities (e.g., relationships with co-workers or membership in loosely organized groups). Still others pertain to very highly patterned types of relationships. Given that marriage operates as a framework for the development of masculinity, men will increase their involvement in more structured relationships, but reduce their involvement in those less structured. The pattern of findings that would be most consistent with the argument about marriage and masculinity would show participation in church and with relatives increasing most and involvement with co-workers and work-related groups less. We would also expect to find that contact with friends or neighbors, participation in sports or hobby clubs, and frequently bars or taverns would actually decline.

One additional series of questions tangential to social contacts is used in this chapter. These deal with the number of hours per week normally spent on various household tasks. My intention is to identify tasks unambiguously identified as housework—done inside the dwelling.[4] This aspect of men's lives is important because husbands' involvement in housework may help explain how and why marriage affects personal communities. To study men's housework, the following are considered: hours per week spent (1) preparing meals, (2) washing dishes, (3) cleaning house, and (4) washing and ironing clothes.

Finding for Transitions into and out of Marriage

I present the findings in this chapter in much the same way I did those for adult achievement. However, rather than consider the consequences of transitions into and out of marriage for the various types of men's personal communities and organizational membership, I will focus on changes due to *marriage only*. (Changes associated with divorce, remarriage, or widowerhood are found in the Appendix tables to this chapter.) This method of presentation makes it possible to examine simultaneously the effects of marriage on many types of social contacts. The purpose of this analysis is to establish that marriage is associated with changes in men's personal communities. But it does not explain why. Once the effects of getting married are considered, I turn attention to an examination of married men to explore the influence of the dimensions of normative marriage developed in the last chapter.

The consequence of marriage refers not to differences between married and unmarried men but to *changes* in men's lives as a result of *changes* in men's marital status. Any consequence, therefore, is the average change associated with marriage once the effects of age have been removed. Since the outcome being measured is change, factors that do not change in men's lives are not relevant. For example, one's race might reasonably be expected to affect patterns of social activities. However, because race cannot vary over time in a man's life, it cannot affect change in any outcome studied.[5]

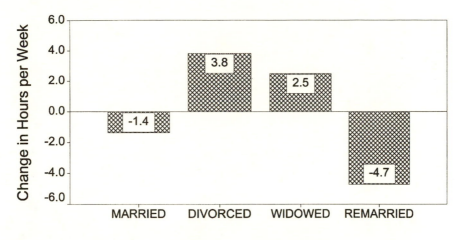

Figure 5.1. *Average change in time spent on housework as a result of changes in marital status.* Data from the National Survey of Families and Households: 1987–1994.

Before we examine men's personal communities, consider briefly husbands' involvement in indoor housework. Figure 5.1 shows that men do *less* housework after they marry. The patterns are consistent, though modest, in revealing reductions in housework following transitions *into* marriage, with comparable increases following transitions *out* of marriage.

The reduction of about 1.4 hours per week caused by a first marriage is the most compelling evidence here because it is unlikely to be the result of responsibilities for children. That is, a first marriage for men is unlikely to reduce responsibilities for children that may include cooking or cleaning. For a small number of men with custody of children after a divorce, a remarriage may reduce or redistribute such responsibilities. Although this is unlikely to be the reason for the large reductions in housework between first marriages and remarriages, it is probably part of it. The overall trends revealed in this graph present compelling evidence that men reduce their efforts in housework when they marry (for the first or subsequent times) and increase them when their marriages end. At this point, it is impossible to examine why marriage has such effects. That will be done in the latter part of this chapter when I turn to the factors in marriage that influence the social communities. It is clear, however, that marriage changes the type of activites men do at home. In a marriage, housework appears to be the wife's work, a finding foreshadowed in earlier chapters. If the household is a gender factory, then one would expect just such a pattern. Once married, men will withdraw from activities culturally defined as "feminine." Whether marriage alters other aspects of social life is the next question.

Now let us consider the more direct measures of social involvement. If men

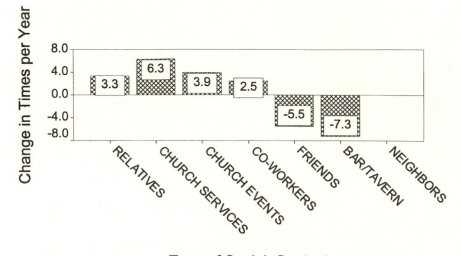

Type of Social Contact

Figure 5.2. *Consequences of marriage for men's social contacts.* Bars are shown only for statistically significant effects. Data from the National Survey of Families and Households: 1987–1994.

reduce their efforts *in* the household once married, are there corresponding changes in their personal networks and memberships in various organizations? Answers to this question appear in the next two graphs. The first presents consequences of marriage for social contacts with others; the second focuses on participation in various types of organizations.

First, consider the changes in men's involvement with relatives, illustrated in Figure 5.2. As I noted earlier, there are practical reasons to expect this to increase (men do, after all, have more relatives after they marry). But the presence of more relatives in the kin group does not necessarily imply greater contact with them, just as it does not necessarily imply cordial relationships. Kinship relationships are governed by strong norms and, as a result, men may increase their involvement once married.

Figure 5.2 shows that marriage does, in fact, increase men's contact with their relatives. Married men report getting together socially with relatives about three more times per year than they did when they were single. Perhaps this is a small change, yet it is only one aspect of men's lives that changes as a result of marriage. Other dimensions of men's social lives change as well. Once such possibilities have been considered, we can put the magnitude of this particular change in better perspective.

Turning now to other highly structured relationships, I focus on the consequence of marriage for various forms of religious involvement (the second and third bars in Figure 5.2). As Figures 5.2 and 5.3 dramatically show, marriage brings

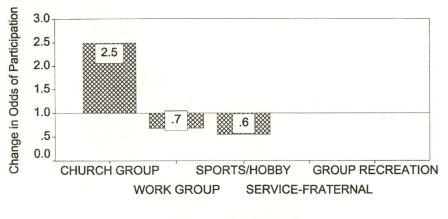

Figure 5.3. *Consequences of marriage for men's organizational involvement.* Bars are shown only for statistically significant effects. Data from the National Survey of Families and Households: 1987–1994.

about an enormous increase in men's involvement with the church. Not only do men attend religious services more often once married (about six more times per year), they also attend social events at synagogue or church about four more times per year. And marriage even influences participation in church-affiliated groups. Once married, the odds that a man will belong to such a group increase 2.5 times. Clearly, involvement with the church is strongly conditioned by marital status.

When attention turns to relationships governed by less structure and rules, the consequences of marriage are as expected. For example, social occasions with co-workers increase minimally after marriage (about 2.5 times more often per year). And membership in work-related organizations (e.g., unions or professional organizations) actually declines somewhat after marriage. The odds that married men will participate in such organizations are only .7 what they were before getting married. Marriage appears to foster greater involvement with the specific individuals a man works with. Co-workers are a part of the workplace itself. Unions or professional societies are organized around the occupation rather than the specific individuals in the place of employment.

Finally, the effect of marriage on the least structured, least normative types of relationships and organizations confirms the general trends already noted. For example, men spend much *less* time with friends outside of the neighborhood once they marry. Such contacts drop by almost six times per year. Husbands appear to form ties with their relatives, congregation members, and co-workers to replace those with other friends. Marriage also brings about a sharp reduction in social evenings at bars or taverns (by over seven times per year). Husbands also *drop* their memberships in informal sports or hobby groups. Compared to bachelors, mar-

ried men have only .60 the odds of participating in such organizations. Only relationships with neighbors, participation in group recreational activities (e.g., bowling), and membership in fraternal or service organizations seem unaffected by
changes in marital status.

Taken together, these results give a consistent image of how men's personal
communities are altered by marriage. Some types of relationships become more
conspicuous; others become less so. Few types of personal ties and memberships
are unaffected. Moreover, the magnitudes and directions of change are consistent
with an explanation based on the gendered nature of marriage. Married men's involvement with others tends to take place in more structured and organized settings, with informal friendships and contacts relegated to lesser importance.

Married Men and Variations in Normative Marriage

We still do not know how or why marriage has these consistent effects on men. As
noted earlier, there are many possible reasons why married life would differ from
the life of a bachelor, some of which are related to the institutional aspects of marriage. To determine whether the dimensions of normative marriage help explain
why men's personal communities alter when they marry. I now turn to an examination of married men. These results are based on the 2,156 married men who
participated in the NSFH in both 1987 and 1993. Wide variation exists among
these men on all dimensions of normative marriage. For example, some have been
married one or two years, whereas others are approaching their golden wedding
anniversary (the longest marriage in this sample of men under age 64 was 46 years).
Some men have no children; others have as many as eight. Some husbands are
completely dependent on their wives' incomes, and others vice versa. Some couples depend entirely on sources of income other than those produced by their employment, whereas others earn all of their income. I now concentrate on how
changes in these dimensions between 1987 and 1993 produced changes in men's
social lives. In conducting such analyses, one can determine whether the consequences of the transition into marriage (discussed above) are the result of the various dimensions of normative marriage. If these aspects of marriage have little or
no consequence, then the changes engendered by getting married are probably unrelated to the normative components of marriage.

The figures in the rest of the chapter are constructed in the same fashion as
those in the previous chapter, with the multivariate results presented in Appendix
B.[6] Only those dimensions of marriage with an effect on a particular type of social contact are represented. For each such dimension, the effects shown would
occur for the maximum amount of change. For example, one dimension of marriage measures maturity by calculating the proportion of a couple's total income
produced by the husband and wife through their combined earnings. This measure ranges from zero to one. In the graphs that follow, the effect of this dimen-

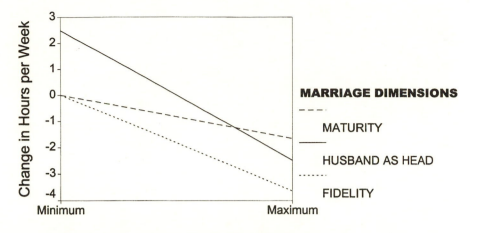

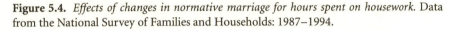

Change from Minimum to Maximum

Figure 5.4. *Effects of changes in normative marriage for hours spent on housework.* Data from the National Survey of Families and Households: 1987–1994.

sion is shown for its changes across its entire range, from minimum (zero) to maximum (one).

Housework

First, let's evaluate the issue of housework. Declines in housework indicate a retreat from traditionally feminine tasks. Figure 5.4 shows the importance of various dimensions of normative marriage in affecting men's involvement in housework.

First, increases in family independence (the measure of maturity) are associated with declines in housework. In other words, as a man's family becomes less dependent on others, his involvement in the "feminine" pursuits of housework drops.

Changes in the relative incomes of husbands and wives also alter a man's housework commitments. Relative income is a measure of the aspect of marriage that holds that the husband is the head of the household. As a man's income increases relative to his wife's, he is less likely to do housework.

Finally, the longer husbands are married to particular women, the less housework they do. The duration of a marriage indexes the idea of fidelity or monogamy. Presumably, the longer a man is married, the more he will come to view the marriage as likely to endure forever. Consequently, men become less involved in the tasks of cooking, cleaning, and laundry. These three findings support the view of a married household as a gender factory. Shifts in marriage toward more traditional patterns (at least in these three dimensions) are associated with declines in men's involvement in housework. Normative marriage, it appears, assigns primary responsibility for such tasks to the wife.

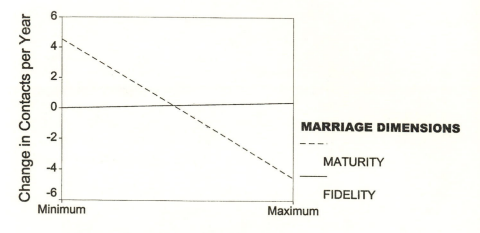

Change from Minimum to Maximum

Figure 5.5. *Effects of changes in normative marriage for social contacts with relatives.* Data from the National Survey of Families and Households: 1987–1994.

Relatives

Turning now to actual measures of relationships and memberships, I consider how marriage affects men's sociable contacts with relatives. As Figure 5.5 illustrates, only two dimensions of marriage influence such contacts. When family income is generated solely by the married couple, contact with relatives actually *declines.* Men who live in families that receive significant amounts of income from sources other than the couple's own earnings, therefore, are more likely to socialize with their relatives. And since it is change that is being measured, the findings imply that when a married couple becomes more self-sufficient, husbands reduce their contacts with kin. Because this measure taps the normative dimension of maturity, one would expect that things might go the other way—greater independence (maturity) leading to greater involvement with kin.

This finding tells us that relationships with relatives are, in fact, bonds of obligation. Of the many sources of family income other than that produced by the married couple, the single largest category is gifts and loans from *relatives*, as the next chapter shows. This being so, these findings describe a common observation in social life: the receipt of something of value puts a person in debt. There is a tension established as a result of a gift that pushes toward reciprocity. Gifts are rarely *not* reciprocated (Caplow, 1982) in some fashion. So long as couples are dependent on others (primarily other kin), therefore, they appear to reciprocate such generosity with social contacts such as dinner or birthday parties, family picnics, or other events.

There is also a very minimal change in contact with relatives as a result of longer durations of marriage. I predicted this measure of fidelity and monogamy would have such an effect, but one should not make too much of this very small change.

Now, a central question is whether the findings just described can explain the shift in contacts with relatives associated with the initial transition to marriage (see Figure 5.2). As already shown, marriage increases such contacts by an average of three or four more times per year. Can this increase be reconciled with the decrease associated with greater financial independence? Indeed, the two findings are quite understandable and complementary. A married couple is most likely to depend on others for income in the early years of marriage, when setting up a house, having children, purchasing furnishings and other requirements of married life (Gove, Grimm, Motz, and Thompson, 1973; Wilenski, 1971). So it is not surprising to have discovered an increase in contact with kin following a first marriage in the past five years because men in such marriages likely depend on others more at this stage of their lives than at later ages. Indeed, the magnitude of change following marriage (increased contact) is virtually the same as the increase associated with high levels of dependence on others for income.

Before we consider involvement in religious organizations, a general issue that pertains to all of the results yet to be presented must be broached. Figure 5.5 shows an effect only for two dimensions of normative marriage, the only two that had statistical effects. As shown in the balance of this chapter, the various dimensions of normative marriage differ in their importance. Whereas shifts toward more normative patterns typically yield expected results, not every aspect of marriage affects a particular type of social contact or membership. In other words, the results show that men respond to differing aspects of their marriage in the construction of their personal communities. In some cases parenthood seems most important, in others, financial independence (maturity) or relative income (husband as head). Men's social networks are built in response to specific changes in their married lives. Marriage is apparently experienced as several discrete, though related, elements. In response to changes in parental status, for example, certain types of social contact increase, but others do not. In response to changes in financial circumstances, likewise, only certain types of memberships are dropped or added. The patterns, if any, of such effects may inform our understanding of how marriage matters to men. I return to this point in the conclusion.

Church

Large and pervasive increases in men's involvement with the church follow marriage. The reasons for such changes can be inferred if one studies the next three figures, which describe attendance at services, participation in social events at church, and membership in church-sponsored organizations.

Figure 5.2 showed that attendance at religious services increased by over six

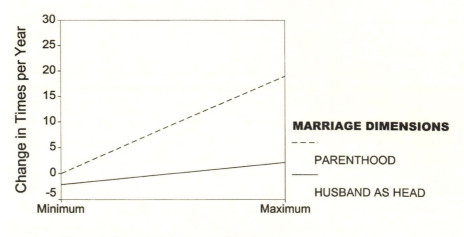

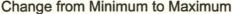

Change from Minimum to Maximum

Figure 5.6. *Effects of changes in normative marriage for church attendance.* Data from the National Survey of Families and Households: 1987–1994.

times per year following a marriage. Other studies have shown that the presence of young children leads to higher rates of church attendance, and the findings illustrated in Figure 5.6 accord with this conclusion (see Gallup and Castilli, 1989: 34–36). Changes in the number of children in the married couple's household have large consequences for men's church attendance (in this chapter, parenthood is measured as change in the number of children). With each additional child, men increase their attendance at services by 2.5 times per year (see Figure 5.6).[7]

Church attendance is also affected by changes in husbands' and wives' relative incomes. If a husband earns more than his wife, his attendance at services increases accordingly. To dramatize the magnitude of such an effect, Figure 5.6 also compares the church or synagogue attendance of a man who once earned no income but now earns all of the couple's income (the maximum possible change). Such a man would attend four more religious services a year as a result. And, of course, shifts in the opposite direction (husband's earnings declining relative to his wife's) would cause a comparable drop in attendance.

Consider next the frequency of participating in social events at church, charted in Figure 5.7. Changes in the number of children in the family are, again, most central. Additional children cause very important consequences for attendance at social events at church or synagogue (about two more per year for each additional child). As others have shown, fathers (and mothers) take their children to events sponsored by their congregation for the moral education and wholesome contacts they afford (Gallup and Castelli, 1989).

Finally, membership in church-affiliated groups such as adult Talmud study clubs, Methodist Men, or outreach ministries is affected by changes in men's fi-

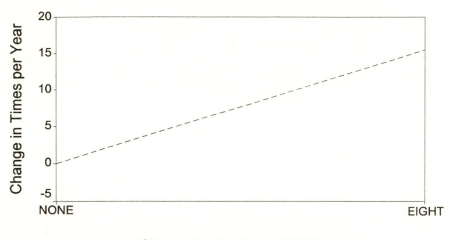

Change in Number of Children

Figure 5.7. *Effects of changes in number of children for social events at church.* Data from the National Survey of Families and Households: 1987–1994.

nancial independence. While greater independence (the measure of maturity) reduced contact with relatives, it has strong positive effects on church-group membership. So, as Figure 5.8 shows, not only do more independent men attend church more frequently, they are also more likely to join church groups. The probability that the hypothetical man just described (whose church attendance increased due to changes in family independence) would join a church group increases by a substantial 16% as a result of changes in his relative income.

The large increases in men's involvement with the church that follow marriage can now be assessed as partly a consequence of the components of normative marriage. The measures of maturity, parenthood, and husband-as-head are all strong factors influencing men's religious involvements.

The magnitude by which marriage influences men's religious involvement is quite impressive. The institution of the church, it appears, is very closely allied with the institution of marriage. And this simple observation may be a clue to a more fundamental principle. I have repeatedly argued that marriage provides a clear template for men. I have also argued that masculinity is associated with an emphasis on rules, structure, and social roles, in opposition to the feminine emphasis on intimacy, unity, and uniqueness. That married men would be so much more likely to participate in a very structured institution like the church, therefore, is telling. There is, indeed, a *very close affinity* between the institutions of religion and the family for men. Family and church are the most traditional social institutions.

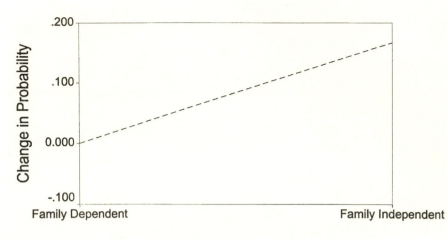

Change from Minimum to Maximum

Figure 5.8. *Effect of changes in family independence on probability of membership in religious organization.* Data from the National Survey of Families and Households: 1987–1994.

Co-workers and Work Organizations

Social contacts with co-workers and memberships in work-related organizations are governed by weaker expectations than those just considered. Because such ties are less institutionalized, one would expect that marriage would produce smaller consequences than those for religious participation. Recall that getting married increased men's involvement with their co-workers but reduced their membership in unions and professional organizations by small amounts (Figures 5.2 and 5.3).

An analysis of how marriage affects these types of contacts offers more insight into why marriage makes a difference. Social contacts with co-workers decline when men have more children. Indeed, the consequence of fatherhood for such contacts is actually quite large when the cumulative effects of additional children are considered (about 1.5 fewer social contacts for each additional child). On the other hand, there are modest increases in social contacts with co-workers that result from improvements in family independence (i.e., maturity). Men respond to one aspect of their marriage by increasing contacts with co-workers, but respond to another by decreasing them—dual tendancies that Figure 5.9 graphically portrays. Not all dimensions of normative marriage are equally important. And not all types of social contact are equally governed by social rules. So the findings about co-workers are what one would expect given the nature of such relationships. If men are to increase significantly their participation in activities such as church and kin contacts, something else is likely to decline.

Little work is required to maintain the ties that unite men through their com-

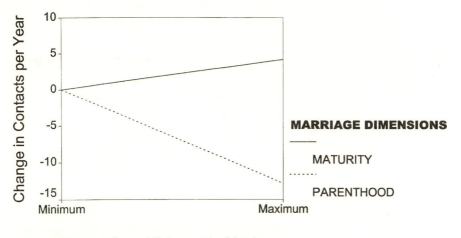

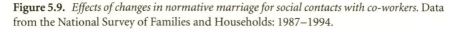

Change from Minimum to Maximum

Figure 5.9. *Effects of changes in normative marriage for social contacts with co-workers.* Data from the National Survey of Families and Households: 1987–1994.

mon employment. Co-workers are connected by their common membership in an organization. Therefore, one would expect that marriage might increase these ties, but not to the same extent as those for such highly structured pursuits as religion. Children, it appears, take priority over any other dimension of marriage, including this type of contact and, possibly, others.

Once they are married, men may spend a little more time socializing with their co-workers, but they are less likely to maintain their memberships in labor unions or other work-related organizations (see Figure 5.3). Analysis of how both happen reflects the marginal importance of such contacts in married men's lives. Several dimensions of marriage influence work-group memberships, but they do so inconsistently. As men's incomes increase relative to their wive's (i.e., husband as head), and as family income becomes more independent of other sources (i.e., maturity), work-related memberships increase. On the other hand, the longer marriages endure and as men's value in the marriage market declines (and the value of his marriage increases), participation declines. In such ways, the various dimensions of marriage compete in their influence on men's social participation, as Figure 5.10 shows.

The previous chapter showed that marriage increases men's commitment to work (married men work more weeks per year and earn more than unmarried men). It is not surprising, therefore, to discover a small increase in social contacts with co-workers. Clearly, however, the pursuit of occupational goals is not a unitary objective. The tangible and symbolic significance of higher incomes and more prestigious positions is clearly more important to men than the less obvious and indirect benefits of belonging to a professional society or labor union.

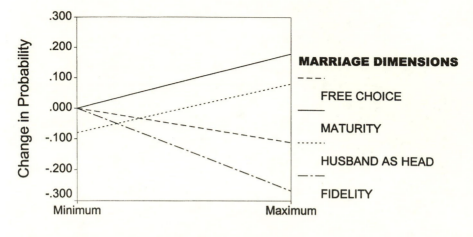

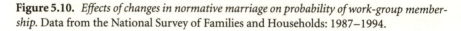

Change from Minimum to Maximum

Figure 5.10. *Effects of changes in normative marriage on probability of work-group membership.* Data from the National Survey of Families and Households: 1987–1994.

Other Relationships

Finally, consider relationships governed by the weakest and fewest social rules: those with friends and neighbors and memberships in various loosely organized clubs. When men marry, there is a drop in contacts with friends, a drop in sports and hobby club membership, and a large drop in social evenings at bars and taverns (see Figure 5.3). Marriage had no effect on contacts with neighbors, group recreational activities, or memberships in fraternal organizations. Why are there declines in the three aspects that respond to marriage (friends, bars and taverns, and sport and hobby club memberships)? Four figures give the answer.

First, the consequence of marriage for friendly social contacts and evenings at bars is related primarily to men's roles as fathers. As Figures 5.11 and 5.12 show, the more children men have in the household, the less time they spend with friends outside the neighborhood and the fewer times per year they go to a bar or a tavern. Married men's roles as fathers appear to take priority over other attributes they derive from their marriages in these respects. Increasing numbers of children lead to higher involvement in religious organizations but to lower levels of contacts with friends and co-workers. Married men, that is, allocate their time differently once they become fathers. Paternity has enormous consequences for increased participation in church. It has large negative consequences for less organized and less structured types of relationships.

Figure 5.13 suggests that the decline in sporting and hobby club memberships that follows marriage appears to be related to the relative earnings of husbands and wives. Men are more likely to drop their memberships in such clubs when

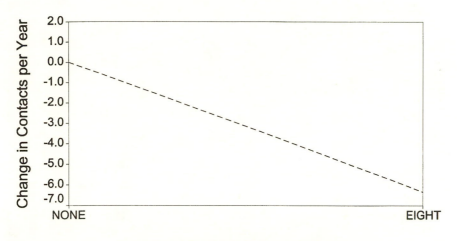

Figure 5.11. *Effects of changes in number of children for social contacts with friends.* Data from the National Survey of Families and Households: 1987–1994.

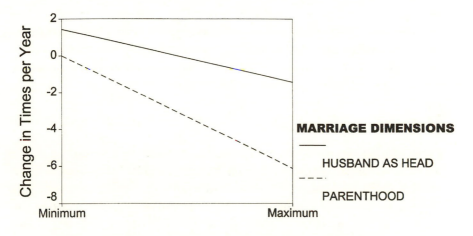

Figure 5.12. *Effects of changes in normative marriage for social evenings at bars/taverns.* Data from the National Survey of Families and Households: 1987–1994.

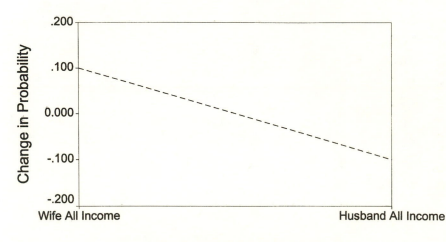

Change in Husband's Relative Income

Figure 5.13. *Effects of changes in relative income on probability of sport/hobby club membership.* Data from the National Survey of Families and Households: 1987–1994.

their own incomes increase relative to their wives', perhaps in favor of other pursuits. Figure 5.14 suggests that one such alternative pursuit may be interacting with neighbors. Although the transition to marriage was not a factor in social contacts with neighbors, changes in ongoing marriages are. The same factor that reduces men's participation in sport and hobby clubs (i.e., an increase in husbands' relative earnings) increases contacts with neighbors.

Change or Re-allocation?

Before concluding, I emphasize one final issue. The foregoing analyses have shown that men respond to changes in their marital status and in their marriages by increasing or reducing contacts with others and memberships in organizations. Since some of the changes following marriage were positive (e.g., involvement with church, kin, or co-workers) whereas others were negative (e.g., reduced contact with friends, membership in work organizations, membership in sports/hobby clubs, evenings at bars), the obvious question is whether men change the *absolute number* of such ties and relationships or whether they simply *re-allocate* and shift their commitments and allegiances from one to another.

To answer such a question, I examined changes in the total number of times per year that men reported doing all of the activities already examined. Here the concern was whether marriage increased, reduced, or had no discernible effect on the total. Some types of changes in marital status have significant consequences for the total number of contacts men reported (summed over all measures). Men who remarried reported about 26 fewer contacts per year, whereas men who divorced

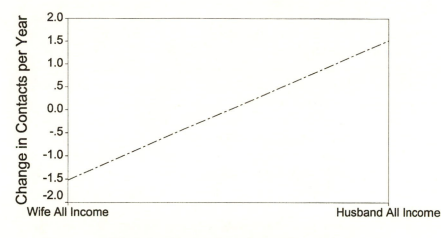

Change in Husband's Relative Income

Figure 5.14. *Effects of changes in relative income for social contacts with neighbors.* Data from the National Survey of Families and Households: 1987–1994.

or became widows reported more (24 and 78, respectively). But getting married, per se, had *no* measurable consequences. Likewise, changes in the dimensions of normative marriage showed no measurable effects.

These findings mean that men maintain relatively constant levels of involvement with their personal communities before and after they get married. Increases in one type of pursuit are accompanied by decreases in another. Marriage, that is, has effects on men because husbands allocate their time and commitments differently. They do not significantly increase or decrease their total commitments.

Conclusion

This chapter began by considering how marriage might affect the people and organizations men are involved with, their personal communities. It is this collection of close friends, relatives, co-workers, and acquaintances that informs a sense of who one is in important ways. At the most personal level, the lives of men are influenced by their associations with others. Such ties, and the ways men experience and respond to them, cross the strong privacy boundaries erected around marriages and families because they are part of a man's sense of himself and his place in the world. To the many factors known to alter men's personal communities, we must now add changes in their marital status and changes in their marriages.

Marriage does not appear to add or subtract so much as it reorganizes the total amount of contact men have with other people. One of the most obvious ways in which men reorganize their time involves work in the household. Once married, men do less housework than they did when they were bachelors. Other changes in personal communities appear consistent with this obvious gendered pattern. Overall, the changes observed in men's social contacts move toward more structure, more normative rules, and relationships more like marriage itself.

The results in this chapter have shown that the dimensions of normative marriage have differing consequences for men. In many cases, one or two dimensions affected social contacts but others had no consequences. Parenthood, however, stood out as a key dimension of marriage that appears to exert greater influence over men's social lives than any other single aspect of normative marriage. Changes in a man's financial circumstances were also important, although somewhat less than parenthood. Husbands' and wives' relative incomes and family independence were both shown to matter for the types of personal communities men make.

The soft boundaries that define the institution of marriage limit the discretion that individual husbands and wives have in creating their positions in it. Once men have embraced marriage, they appear to organize much of the rest of their lives in similar constructions. Married men are much more likely to be active members of a church or synagogue. They attend services more frequently, participate in social events at church, and join organizations sponsored by their congregations. They expand their contacts with relatives (at least early in their marriages). They spend more social time with their co-workers. Despite the obvious differences among these diverse types of pursuits, each resembles marriage in being surrounded by convention and custom. At church, with relatives, and with co-workers, there are clear norms of propriety, standards of conduct that inhere in the relationships themselves. Little work is required to create or sustain such relationships. Each depends on a common membership in an organization (work) or institution (family).

A man may change the church he attends, may change jobs, or may acquire new members of his extended family. But such changes are not likely to alter the rules that govern his encounters in those contexts. His relationships in all such cases are structured by his membership. All that is required to maintain (or create) relationships in these contexts is his adequate participation in them. So long as he is married, he acquires relatives. So long as he is employed, he acquires co-workers. And so long as he is a member of his church, he acquires fellow congregants. Even if he changes jobs, this will not change. He will probably treat his new co-workers much as he did his old ones. If he socializes with co-workers in his old job, he will socialize with his co-workers in his new job. At his new church, he will probably act much as he did in his old church. And when a new member joins the larger kin group through marriage or birth, his relations with that person will resemble those with others who share the same position. Married men appear to focus their personal communities around positions rather than specific, particular, individuals. Husbands interact with other members of their congregations *as* members of those congregations. Husbands socialize with co-workers *as* co-workers.

If these assertions are true, we may say that a man's relationships in such settings are *roles*. There is a way to act when one is someone's manager. There is a way to act when one is a lay leader in a church. And there is a way to act toward one's niece or sister-in-law. And, of course, there is a way to act as a husband. These "ways" are the conventions, or expectations, attached to each such role. Married men's personal networks appear to be constructed through memberships and scripted patterns rather than through more intimate personal connections.

The associations and contacts that have been discussed are quite diverse in ways that go beyond their relative degrees of structure and normative content. Others who study this issue have identified several additional ways to distinguish among them. Some researchers contrast *instrumental or purposive* with *expressive or solidary* associations to draw attention to the distinction between those aimed mainly at some tangible outcome for the participant, or for some client or group (the former), and those in which participation itself is the main source of satisfaction. A related scheme focuses on the relative importance of *self* versus *community* orientations (Janoski and Wilson, 1995). This perspective directs our attention to the relative importance of advancing an individual's self-interests versus the goal of improving some community. For example, professional societies, labor unions, or veterans' groups are self-oriented. The primary (though not only) reason for participating is to advance one's own interests—even if that means nothing more than friendly association with other people. The same can be said of sports and hobby clubs. On the other hand, religious organizations, neighborhood associations, and service organizations are community-oriented. Men undoubtedly derive personal gratification from memberships in them. But the primary goal of each is to improve a community. This framework portrays the consequences of normative marriage as increasing the amount of community-oriented endeavors at the expense of self-oriented pursuits. *Real* men are generous in obvious ways—the topic of the next chapter.

The guiding assumptions about marriage and masculinity tell us that social participation is a form of gender display (presentation of self) for men. By the choices they make in creating a personal community, husbands construct a public identity or reputation. The man who openly and publicly commits himself to others, especially *communities of others*, is saying something about the type of person he is. His energies are openly directed toward the world of other people. No matter how steadfast and loving he may be in his family roles, such a man is also announcing his commitment to things *outside* his family. If masculinity is defined in opposition to femininity, then such a statement is essential. Femininity has traditionally been associated with the world of private affairs, family life, home and children—historically the principal domains of women.

In these ways, married men's behaviors make sense. By emphasizing relationships governed by rules and normative structure, men reject or abandon the more traditional feminine traits of empathy, intimacy, and close interpersonal unity. In doing so, they conform to conventional standards of masculinity.

NOTES

1. The NSFH is not a simple random sample. For various reasons, the design included oversamples of certain racial and marital-status groups (e.g., blacks newly married and cohabiting couples). To correct for such intentional nonrepresentativeness, sample weights are applied to render the results generalizable to the entire nation. However, since the sample weights are, themselves, a function of factors included as independent variables, unweighted OLS regression produced essentially identical results (Winship and Radbill, 1994).

2. It is possible with NSFH to establish precise dates for each transition ("relationship term" in NSFH terminology). However, when such interval lags were included in equations estimating consequences of marital transitions, there were no average effects. This suggests that whatever consequences were revealed are enduring and resistant to change over the short time period represented in these data.

3. In Wave 1, the questions about spending social time were asked with slightly different wording, preceded by "Spend a social evening" rather than "Get together socially." For the questions about group memberships, Wave 1 asked specifically about each type mentioned, whereas Wave 2 combined several in each question. For purposes of comparability, I created measures from Wave 1 that included the same categories mentioned in Wave 2. For example, for the question about service clubs, fraternal groups, or political groups, I used the one with the most frequent participation. I did not average or otherwise combine the various questions. This gave the highest possible level of membership participation to each individual in Wave 1.

4. Several other items were also included, such as "shopping" or "paying bills." However, it is not entirely certain that these are done in the home. Other tasks were unambiguously done outside the house. One question dealt with outdoor home maintenance, and another with auto maintenance. These were the only two items done entirely outside the house. Therefore, while it was possible to construct a measure for the performance of housework, it was not possible to construct a measure for the performance of things outside the house. It should be noted, however, that outdoor maintenance efforts increased after marriage—the opposite of what happened for indoor housework. On the other measure of outdoor effort, there was no measurable consequence of marriage. Such changes, however, may reflect the higher rate of home ownership among married than single men (i.e., purchasing a home would probably increase a man's maintenance efforts compared with those done while he was renting an apartment.

5. The equations estimated included lagged values for all dependent and independent variables. In addition, dummys for race (White, Hispanic, Other) were initially included, as were continuous variables for educational attainment and age. The inclusion of race and education (factors unlikely to change) was in recognition of the possibility that average changes might vary by race or education. However, this did not occur. All equations for marital transitions, therefore, were estimated with controls for age only. Specification issues are of much less concern when attention is focused on changes within individual records rather than on differences among comparable individuals. The inclusion of background factors makes little or no difference in such equations unless such factors are correlated with the magnitude of change over time.

6. To represent the effects of changes in dimensions of marriage on group member-

ships, I present the results of logistic regressions in terms of changes in probabilities to make the graph lines easier to plot. The whole equations are found in Appendix B.

7. To represent the frequency of contacts and participation levels, responses of "never" were coded zero. Responses of "several times a year" were coded as 3. Responses of "about once a month" were coded as 10. Responses of "about once a week" were coded as 48. And responses of "several times a week" were coded as 100. Because means and variances of measures of social participation differed in the two waves, I standardized responses within waves by computing the mean and standard deviation of the sum of all items within each wave. Then, each individual item was expressed as a deviation (z-score) from the total average for that wave. The effect is to express participation levels in each wave as a number of standard deviations from the average for that wave. Regressions using such deviation scores were essentially the same as those using raw scores in relative magnitude and direction of effects. To express deviation scores in a frequency metric, I multiplied the regression coefficient by the time-2 standard deviation of the sum of all contacts per year.

Unlike the analysis in the previous chapter, here I study parenthood by considering the number of children rather than the initial transition to parenthood. This was done because the NSFH is a nationally representative sample spanning the entire range of married mens' ages. In the last chapter, all men were under 36. In this chapter, however, there is much greater variation in age. Therefore, the *initial* transition to parenthood occurs very seldomly among members of the sample.

✦ 6 ✦

When Men Help Others

Americans gave over $129 billion to charitable causes in 1995. Roughly 8 of every 10 of these dollars were given by private individuals, not foundations, corporations, or other organizations. Almost 7 in 10 American households (69%) gave some amount of money to charities or other philanthropic causes in 1995. Religious organizations were the primary recipient of Americans' generosity, with health causes, human services, programs for youth, and education receiving the next largest amounts, respectively (Independent Sector, 1996: 1–4) The average contributing American household gave $1,017 to various causes in 1995, or a little over 2% of household income. These amounts are impressive, but they are also an understatement because they do not include gifts to friends or relatives. Nor do they include gifts in kind. Over half of Americans (56%) gave money to relatives or friends in 1995. The total average amount given to such individuals exceeded the amount given to charities by over $500 ($1,527 in 1995; Independent Sector, 1996: Table 4.9). That such a large percentage of Americans makes annual donations suggests clearly that we are a generous people with our money. Much less clear, however, is *why* we give so much.

Some clues to this question appear in various traits known to be associated with giving. For example, family income affects the amount and likelihood that people will give. The more affluent are the most likely to give to charities. However, relative giving (as a percentage of family income) follows a "U-shaped" pattern. Those with the lowest incomes *and* those with the highest contribute a greater percentage of their total family income each year. But those in the middle part with a smaller portion of their incomes. Age is also known to influence giving. As people grow older, they are more likely to give to others. And since most charitable giving is done through churches, it is not surprising to learn that church attendance and strength of religious beliefs are very strongly related to giving (Auten and Rudney, 1989; Chiswick, 1991; Hodgkinson and Weitzman, 1990; Hodgkinson, Weitzman, and Kirsch, 1990). Such patterns tell us something about which people give, but little about what giving means, or why people do it. In this chapter I investigate the role of marriage in fostering generosity. I ask whether men are more or less likely to give to others after they marry. I also investigate how changes in their marriages affect the amounts they give and the targeted beneficiaries of their generosity.

The Meaning of Giving

No matter how simple the act, giving has complicated meanings. For example, a gift is often intended to help the recipient, whether an individual or an organization. But giving also has important implications for the *giver*. At a minimum, a gift establishes an asymmetrical social relationship between the donor and the recipient that most people recognize. Something is expected when a gift is given, even if nothing more than an expression of gratitude. Saying thanks may suffice to balance the exchange by making the donor feel good and discharging any further expectation on the part of the recipient. But more may be called for. Gifts to individuals (and especially kin) are typically reciprocated with gifts of comparable *value* (Caplow, 1982; Wuthnow, 1991).

Anthropologists have found that extensive networks of giving and receiving are integral features of all cultures. Such exchanges are the means by which networks are built and sustained, obligations incurred and discharged, honor bestowed and recognized, and all the groups into which people sort themselves maintained. By giving to this but not that person or group, an individual makes a choice about which relationships or connections matter, and which ones don't. As members of any society give to and receive from one another, the bonds that unite them, and the divisions that separate them, are built and sustained.

Giving may also carry personal moral connotations, especially when the recipient is in obvious need. Our kinship system is an extensive network of very strong obligations linking parents to children and vice versa at differing stages of the life course. Morally, religiously, and legally, parents simply *must* give to their children. Likewise, adult children are expected to give to their parents when the need arises. The parent or child who reneges on these kinship duties will be called upon to account for his actions because such obligations are very clearly understood and shared by most people. The parent who neglects his or her child is newsworthy. Such cases are sufficiently rare to occupy prominent places in our media. Likewise, the obligation to parents is so embedded that *most American adults care for an elderly parent* at some point in their lives (Brody, 1984). The enduring bonds of family obligations are clearly woven of countless "gifts" of money, help, advice, and comfort.

A focus on the importance of obligations orients our thinking about gifts to the future—reciprocal obligations unite and sustain family groups over time. But another perspective locates the meaning of the gift in the immediate moment of the act. Sociologist Robert Wuthnow examined the motives and justifications for *acts of compassion* in his analysis of American individualism (1991). He found that giving is not always associated with duty or obligation. Instead, it is often justified as something that makes a person *feel good.* Personal fulfillment, in other words, may be an important dimension of helping and giving to others. As Wuthnow explained, fulfillment may be the end point; helping people may be merely the means to attaining that end. Wuthnow's subjects explained it this way: "I don't do this to help people. I do it to make myself feel good about helping people.... If I help somebody ... I do that because I want to feel good. It gives me that feeling that I've done something good...." (1991: 96). This raises an interesting question *What is the good feeling that comes from giving?*

In a clever series of experiments and analyses, Wuthnow found that the feeling is not one of sacrifice. Nor is giving, per se, central to self-esteem. Helping other people is not ranked highly among the things that make most Americans feel good about themselves. Rather, fulfillment seems to *precede* rather than *derive* from helping, at least for many. Giving, in other words, may be a form of instant gratification, a dimension of individualism. As one subject explained: "To be able to care for other people, you have to have your own strength. You make a poor helper if you're a weak person" (1991: 108). That is, to give to another presupposes a level of self-confidence, inner strength, and a clear sense of personal identity: "It is this self-confidence that allows one to give" (1991: 114).

According to this perspective, giving issues from, and reinforces, inner strength. It feels good because it tells the donor something about himself. It validates a personal sense of active effectiveness, independence, personal mastery, and competence. He who *can* give to others confirms these things about *himself* in the process, regardless of the benefits that others may derive.

The instant personal benefits are not the only ones. Giving may also confer honor, esteem, respect, and reputation. The philanthropist is remembered for his or her generosity, the selfless volunteer celebrated for the help he gives to others. The conspicuous gift of money is rewarded by public recognition. Buildings are named for the benefactor, academic chairs named for the individual or family who made the bequest that supports them, and foundations named for the one who established the original endowment.

Giving and receiving establish and maintain the informal contracts among people that we recognize as society or personal communities. Such acts, both large and small, define each of us in obvious and subtle ways. We come to know ourselves and others, in part, through such exchanges. We measure our commitment, and that of those around us, partly in the meter of exchanges. Implicitly, to give anything is to give some part of oneself. In doing so, one alters the bonds involved. In a very real sense, the individual about whom we may say "I owe him nothing, and he owes me nothing" is not a part of our personal community in any real sense.

Exchange and the Family

These comments have an obvious bearing on our understanding of marriage and kinship. Although kinship may consist of many other things, one dimension universally recognized by all who study the subject is the *exchange of help* (see Rossi and Rossi, 1990, for a discussion). Indeed, it is possible to map individuals' understandings of their kinship bonds by examining such exchanges.

A classroom exercise intended to help students define the term *family* involves drawing a line down the middle of a sheet of paper. On the left side students write the names of all persons to whom they could appeal for help knowing that it would be given, even if grudgingly. On the right they place the names of all persons who could make the same appeal to them. Then they cross out any name that appears on only one side of the paper. The result, in virtually every case, is a list of people the student defines as his or her *family*. The point is to illustrate how the bonds of kinship are expressed as reciprocal binding obligations to help (Nock, 1992). To give and receive are core expectations of our family institution. Where those obligations exist, people are recognized as relatives, and where they don't, people are not. Marriage, therefore, should have consequences for structuring such obligations for men. It should affect the people men give to (and receive from).

One of the universal dimensions of adult masculinity is the expectation that men will provide for and protect their families. The last chapter showed that such expectations extend beyond the immediate nuclear family to include other relatives. Once married, a man becomes a member of an extensive network of obligations that is wider than it was when he was single. As a husband, he is now expected to accord his family (and relatives) the help they may need. To do so is to play one of the basic scripts of marriage for men. To do otherwise is to fail in that role.

Providing for his relatives and helping out in times of need are expectations for married men. But when a husband does such things, he is also engaging in a form of *gender display*. We know that married men have higher incomes, work more, and have better jobs. Such accomplishments are rightly seen as elements of provision for and support of the family. But they may also be a kind of statement the man is making about himself. Likewise, the husband who gives *conspicuously* to others, and especially to those he is *not* obligated to because of his marriage, is openly showing what kind of man he is.

In the last chapter I showed that marriage fosters greater involvement in the church, with relatives, and in organizations with clear membership criteria. Giving is also known to be related to such patterns. First, membership in a religious congregation is known to lead to much greater giving. But membership in other organizations has similar consequences. People who have extensive personal communities, especially those with organizational connections, give more than people without such networks (Independent Sector, 1996: 92).

There is also the personal dimension of giving. For men to give is to affirm certain core elements of their identities. Giving builds and sustains the efficacy and independence associated with the masculine self-concept. It is a statement about a man's ability to give—his independence and maturity. So, beyond the importance of giving as gender display, such acts are also an *affirmation* of masculinity. Giving may be part of a man's gender identity.

There is some indirect evidence that men, in fact, act this way. Married men appear to give more to charities and causes than unmarried men do. National surveys by the Independent Sector, a Washington, D.C., organization devoted to promoting and studying this issue, show that the average amount of money contributed by married people is about twice that of their unmarried counterparts (average annual giving of $1,298 versus $557 in 1995; 1996: Appendix D, Table 4). Unfortunately, these results do not allow one to distinguish between giving by husbands and giving by wives. More persuasive is the finding that large gifts (over $500) other than those to churches are more likely to come from married than unmarried persons. Married people are 20% more likely than single people to make such donations (1994: 12).

Information about Giving

Information about giving is taken from the same sources used in the last chapter. The NSFH asked all those interviewed to report the amounts they had given to various categories of other people in the last year. This makes it possible to compare giving at two time points. It also makes it possible to investigate the possibility that marriage affects the amounts of giving and persons men give money to. Finally, one can study the consequences of changes in men's marriages. Unfortunately, there are also some important limitations to what can be done with this information.

First, the questions about giving pertain *only* to other people and not to organizations (e.g., churches, schools, or charities). This makes it impossible to investigate the overtly public types of gifts typically known as philanthropy. While unfortunate, the information available is more directly pertinent to our concerns because it pertains to a wide variety of kin and nonkin categories. Marriage likely affects giving to relatives and friends more obviously than to organized charities and causes. Still, given what has been shown about marriage and involvement with the church, it is unfortunate that this provocative question cannot be investigated.

Another limitation of the data is that they provide information only about gifts of more than $200 at one time, an understandable methodological strategy from the perspective of survey research. When interviewed about events in the past year, people are prone to serious errors of recall about small matters. For most Americans, a gift of $200 or more, however, is memorable. Many such gifts would not likely be forgotten, even if the amount involved was remembered incorrectly (e.g., remembering a $300 gift to one's niece when, in fact, the wedding gift was $250). By restricting questions in this way, the researchers traded some specificity for greater accuracy.

Finally, also important, gifts from married couples are not always *individual* decisions. In fact, when a man gives money to a relative, friend, or co-worker, he and his wife likely have conferred about the matter and the amount. The fungible nature of household income makes it difficult to say that a gift is from a husband or from a wife, despite how it is presented or received. Thus, when a man reports that a gift of $500 was made to his spouse's parent, it is not really sensible to view this as a gift from *him* any more than it is to view it as a gift from *his wife*. Gifts emanating from the married couple are corporate gifts in a real sense. They are drawn on the account of both spouses, even if only one makes the donation, even if only one earns the income that makes it possible.

The corporate nature of gifts from married couples means that husbands and wives often share their consequences. But it does not necessarily mean that they share the *same* consequences or that they share them *equally*. The same gift may have very different meanings to a man and his wife. For him, the gift may discharge some sense of filial duty, kinship loyalty, or obligation. Or it may be an expression of his desire for recognition, accomplishment, or success. It may also have these meanings for his wife. But it may not. There is no way of knowing what gifts mean to the people who give them, nor is it necessary to know for the purposes of this research.

We should recognize, however, that gifts from married couples are a different type of behavior than the other issues studied in this book. They are *joint products* in a way that success and personal communities aren't. A man may be constrained by his wife and family in the hours he works, the job he holds, the friends he sees, or the organizations he belongs to. But *his* role in making decisions about each of these areas of his life is greater than *theirs*. He has more discretion in these matters than they do. This may not be as true when it comes to giving money.

As the issue of giving by married men is pursued, bear in mind that gifts are not, strictly speaking, his (or his wife's) alone. One might even be tempted to think of gifts from married couples as the consequence of a wife's choices. Might it be that any change in men's giving associated with marriage is because wives make such decisions? The stingy bachelor may not change at all once he gets married. Perhaps he parts with any of his (their) money only because his wife insists. Even if sometimes true, such logic is probably flawed for the same reason one cannot think of gifts as the husband's alone. The point is that resources that flow from a married couple cannot easily be distinguished as the husband's or the wife's.

A marriage creates a new entity that blurs individual identities for certain legal and social purposes (e.g., tax or injury liability, credit or blame for children's successes and failures). This becomes very clear in the issue of giving. So how is one to make sense of giving by men when, in fact, such actions are corporate (family) decisions? We must view decisions about giving as joint products of the marriage.

Even though I am interested in how marriage affects *men*, a corporate view of family giving is not really much of a problem, for a jointly produced marriage is, after all, a large part of a husband's self-concept. The products of marriage (success and personal communities) have been studied in this book. Now we confront the most obvious instance of such products. Because the guiding assumption of the research is that marriage creates and sustains personal (gender identity) and public (presentation of self) masculine identities, there is no reason to dismiss wives' roles in the construction of their marriages. If married men give more money than single men, then this is logically a consequence of their marriages, and wives are a very large part of the story.

However, there is one way in which the corporate nature of gifts matters for this research. Changes that may be associated with transitions into, or out of, marriage will be more difficult to interpret because such transitions also mean changes in the inherent nature of any gifts given. Before he marries, a man's donations are largely his own affair. Immediately after marriage, however, this changes. Now, they are joint decisions. And immediately after divorce, things change again. For this reason, any changes in giving that are associated with changes in marital status *may* reflect the consequence of marriage as I have defined it (i.e., the normative expectations of the institution). But they may also reflect more basic changes in how decisions are made, how resources are pooled, and how immediate needs (e.g., housing and transportation) are supplied.

Interpretative difficulties pertain less to changes *within* marriages. When I consider how shifts to more or less normative patterns in men's marriage are associated with changes in their giving, the implications are clearer because there is no change in the meaning of the gift in most such cases. Even if the birth of an additional child means more demands on family finances, it does not inherently change the corporate nature of gifts from the married couple the way marriage or divorce does. Before and after the birth, gifts are still joint products. But before and after the marriage, they aren't.

Measuring Gifts and Loans

The source of information for this chapter is a series of questions that asked men to report on gifts and loans. Specifically, each man was asked the following question:

> In the last 12 months, have you given a gift worth more than $200 at any one time to anyone, including sons or daughters, not living with you at the time? Include gifts of items such as a car, furniture, jewelry or stocks as well as gifts of money.

Those who answered "Yes" were asked to report the amount and to whom each gift was made. Answers were recorded as falling onto the following categories: (1)

his parent(s), (2) his mother-in-law or father-in-law (or partner's parent, for co-habiting individuals), (3) his brother or sister, (4) his spouse's brother or sister, (5) his grandparent(s), (6) his spouse's grandparent(s), (7) his child, (8) his spouse's child, (9) grandchild, (10) other relative, and (11) nonrelative.[1]

After the questions about gifts, each man answered comparable questions about loans, with answers recorded in the same fashion (i.e., by category of recipient). In the analyses that follow, gifts and loans are treated separately. It is not entirely clear what a loan represents, unlike a gift. On one hand, it may be that loans substitute for gifts under certain circumstances. When asked for assistance, a man may believe he is unable to give it completely, even if he might be able to loan it. However, one difference seems quite clear: gifts may be solicited by a request for them, but loans are almost always solicited. One rarely makes a loan unless asked. The analysis of loans, therefore, provides some insight into how men deal with requests for help from others.

The issue of asking for help is part of a larger matter that deserves brief discussion. Research has shown that the giving of help (both money and in-kind) is influenced by the relative economic positions of the donor and recipient, at least between generations. Parents are more likely to give help to their less affluent children. And lower-income children are more likely to give help and assistance to parents than higher-income children (Rossi and Rossi, 1990). The reasons for such patterns are matters of speculation, but they raise an important point. The giving of money or gifts is probably influenced by the circumstances of the intended recipient. Relatives and friends who are most needy may receive more than those who are better off. Although probably true, I do not intend to deal with this issue explicitly.

For one reason, it is not feasible to determine the circumstances of recipients because such information is not available. Even if it were, however, there is little reason to think that such information would alter the findings in this chapter. Marriage probably *creates* need by creating more relatives. Even if that need is the reason men's behaviors change, this in no way diminishes the importance of marriage. In essence, I am saying that the network of persons who (possibly) need help, which may arise because of marriage, is part of marriage. If changes in men's behaviors are attributed to changes in their marriages when, in fact, they are the result of an increase in networks of kin, marriage is simply being defined in its broadest sociological sense, as it has been throughout this book.

The Extent of Giving

To put things into proper perspective, it should be noted that giving of the magnitude considered here (i.e., $200 or more) is fairly rare. Among the 3,768 men who participated in both waves of the NSFH, only one in five (23%) gave any gift of $200 or more in the preceding year (1993). Of such gifts, 4 in 10 (42%) were to children and about 1 in 10 (11%) were to nonrelatives. No other single category of recipient was mentioned by more than 10% of men in the study.[2]

Since giving to children dominates all giving, separate analyses were conducted that first excluded, and then included, gifts to children. This was necessary in order to investigate the larger range of kinship and nonkin linkages related to gifts. Differences will be noted. The analysis used the following groups of recipients for both gifts and loans: (1) all kin except children; (2) all kin including children; (3) all nonkin (friends and co-workers).

Findings for Transitions into and out of Marriage

The results of analyses of giving are presented in the same format used in earlier chapters. I first consider the consequences of transitions into and out of marriage in the past five years. Then I turn to a consideration of married men only and examine the consequences of shifts to more or less normative patterns in their marriages. Details of the multivariate analysis are reported in Appendix C.

Gifts to Relatives

There is no graph for gifts made to relatives because recent marital transitions do not appear to have immediate consequences for them. Neither marriage nor divorce (or any other transition) significantly changes the flow of gifts to kin. Getting married, per se, is clearly not a stimulus for greater gifts to relatives in the first few years, despite the fact that marriage creates many new types of such individuals (e.g., in-laws, nieces, nephews, etc.).

Gifts to Nonrelatives

Although recent changes in marital status do not affect men's gifts to relatives, they certainly matter for gifts to nonrelatives. As Figure 6.1 shows, transitions into marriage are associated with reductions in the amount of such gifts, whereas transition out of marriage has the opposite effect. Newly married men gave an average of about $1,875 (in 1993 dollars) less to friends, co-workers, and associates than they did before they married. Men who remarry also reduce such gifts, although by smaller amounts (about $1,050). Recently divorced men, however, now give more (about $1,275) to people they are not related to than they did while married. Like comparable figures in other chapters, bars above the horizontal line indicate increases, and bars below the line indicate reductions in gifts as a result of changes in marital status.

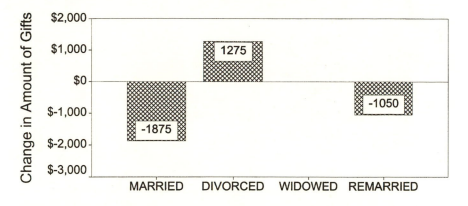

Change in Marital Status

Figure 6.1. *Change in amount of gifts to non relatives as a result of changes in marital status.* All values are in constant 1993 dollars. Bars are shown only for significant effects. Data from the National Survey of Families and Households: 1987–1994.

Loans to Relatives

There are large and significant changes in the amounts men loan to their relatives as a result of getting married. As Figure 6.2 shows, men who recently married make about $2,603 more in loans per year to relatives than they did while single.

The opposite is true when it comes to people men are not related to. Figure 6.3 illustrates how loans to nonrelatives dropped after marriage or remarriage, but increased after divorce or widowhood. In short, transitions into marriage reduced loans and gifts to nonrelatives, but transitions out of marriage generally increased them.

These results in direction and magnitude consistently show that transitions *into* marriage are associated with smaller transfers to nonrelatives, but larger ones to relatives (at least as loans). Transitions *out* of marriage have opposite effects.

Before moving on to variations in the normative dimensions of mens' marriages, recall the point I made earlier about interpreting changes in giving or loaning that are associated with changes in marital status. If gifts and loans are thought to be corporate products of the marriage, then changes in marital status also change this aspect of gifts. Single men have more discretion than married men in their decisions about such matters. For that reason, any conclusions about the effects of marital status changes should be tentative. Those patterns just revealed may reflect the consequences of marriage as a normative institution, but they may also reflect more prosaic and rudimentary aspects of life. Gifts to nonrelatives may drop after marriage because a husband's standard of living consumes more of his income than a bachelor's does, for example. It is difficult to imagine how the routine life of a newly married couple might have the consistent types of effects just seen. Still,

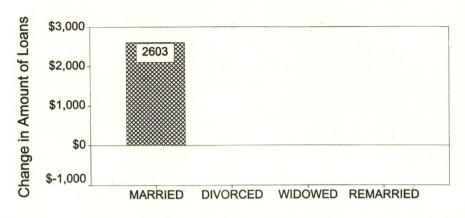

Figure 6.2. *Change in amount of loans to relatives as a result of changes in marital status.* All values are in constant 1993 dollars. Bars are shown only for significant effects. Data from the National Survey of Families and Households: 1987–1994.

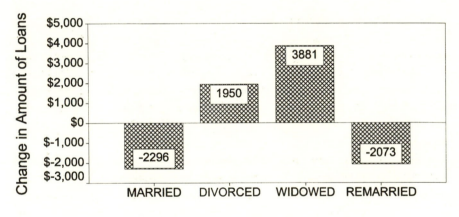

Figure 6.3. *Change in amount of loans to nonrelatives as a result of changes in marital status.* All values are in constant 1993 dollars. Data from the National Survey of Families and Households: 1987–1994.

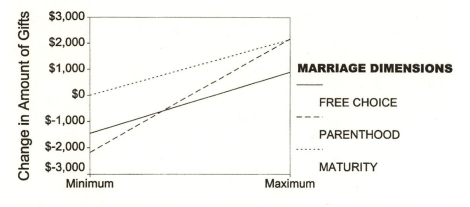

Change from Minimum to Maximum

Figure 6.4. *Effects of changes in normative marriage on amounts of gifts to relatives.* All values are in constant 1993 dollars. Data from the National Survey of Families and Households: 1987–1994.

until variations in men's marriages have been considered, the results just presented should be viewed tentatively.

Married Men and Variations in Normative Marriage

Variations in the normative dimensions of men's marriages can be studied to resolve these sorts of questions. If giving varies in response to changes in a man's marriage, then it is more plausible that the pattern of results just found, in fact, reflects the institutional nature of American marriage, not the more mundane aspects of daily life associated with it. As I show, the findings about married men are entirely consistent with those for transitions into and out of marriage. In fact, the consequences of changes in men's marriages amplify and clarify marriage's effects.

Gifts to Relatives

Because getting married appears to foster greater generosity toward relatives, it would make sense that shifts toward more normative patterns in marriage would produce similar effects. As Figure 6.4 shows, this is exactly what was found. Not every aspect of marriage influences giving, and the magnitudes of effects vary among the dimensions. Nonetheless, the direction of effects is consistent and the magnitudes large.

As I have done in other chapters, I represent the possible effects of shifts in marriage dimensions by showing the consequence of moving from the least to the most normative level of each one. Thus, for example, for the aspect of family independence (maturity), the effects shown represent the result of going from complete dependence on others (no family income produced by earnings of the couple) to complete independence (all family income produced by earnings of the couple). As the graph shows, such a change was found to increase gifts to relatives by about $2,150.

One might argue that such findings reflect little more than the *ability* to give. Clearly, when family income is comprised mainly of sources other than the married couple's earnings, the couple is the *recipient* of some amount of money, but that does not necessarily mean deprivation or shortage. It may simply mean that there are other earners in the family. Likewise, to earn every cent of family income does not mean affluence. Even those with very meager family incomes may earn all of it. Still, it is reasonable to reserve judgment until other dimensions of marriage have been examined.

Changes in the number of children are also associated with changes in gifts to relatives. Each additional child leads to an average increase of about $544 in gifts to relatives. Although few married couples would see an increase or decrease of four children in five years, this is the actual range of fertility differences found in the national sample. Recall that the number of children is determined by counting the number of biological offspring living in the household. In the course of five years, children move in and out of the house. As a result of births and changes in residence, changes of this magnitude are possible, although unusual.

The measure of free choice (i.e., age-specific sex ratio) is also a factor in giving gifts to relatives. Over the entire range of actual changes, increases in the value of marriage are associated with increases of $2,347 in gifts to relatives. This measure, of course, sometimes drops and sometimes rises, depending on a particular man's age in a particular year. For that reason, the plotted values originate below the horizontal line, indicating that a decline in the market value of the marriage would be associated with a decline in gifts to relatives as well.

These results are consistent in showing how various changes in marriage are associated with increased giving to relatives. Giving to one's kin does not seem to be influenced by changes in husbands' and wives' relative incomes (husband as head) or how long couples have been married (fidelity/monogamy). On the other hand, family independence (maturity), market value (free choice), and parenthood influence giving to relatives in ways one would expect.

Gifts to Nonrelatives

Getting married was shown to be associated with a reduction in the amount given to people who are not relatives (see Figure 6.1). However, there is little evidence that *changes in marriage* are responsible for this. In other words, the dimensions of normative marriage do not appear to be related to changes in gifts to nonrelatives. The only evidence found on this matter showed small negative consequences for

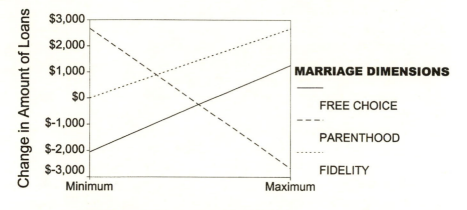

Change from Minimum to Maximum

Figure 6.5. *Effects of changes in normative marriage on amount of loans to relatives.* All values are in constant 1993 dollars. Data from the National Survey of Families and Households: 1987–1994.

additional children in the household. That evidence, however, was not sufficiently strong to be statistically significant. So whatever is responsible for reductions in such gifts is unrelated to the institutional aspects of marriage as I have measured them. It may be the increased demands on income, the change in decision making, or some other elementary aspect of daily life associated with matrimony that matters. So, even though normative marriage clearly makes a difference in giving to relatives, it does not appear to have much consequence for gifts to others.

Loans to Relatives

Shifts toward more normative patterns in marriage also help explain loans to relatives. Loans and gifts, however, appear to be different types of transfers, as we see by comparing the following results with the comparable graph for gifts (see Figure 6.4). For both types of transfers, changes in the market value of the marriage (free choice) have large and notable consequences. Beyond this, however, there is an obvious difference that may illuminate how these two categories of money are treated by married people.

The most telling finding in Figure 6.5 is the *negative effect* of additional children. Each additional child reduces loans to relatives by about $668, despite the positive effect of longer marriages. In other words, as marriages endure, loans to relatives increase somewhat. But this effect is more than canceled by any additional children a couple might have. When the results for *gifts* to relatives (already presented) are compared with those for loans, it is clear that additional children are associated with greater gifts, but smaller loan transfers. Why?

I noted earlier that the analyses were conducted twice, once for gifts to relatives except children and again for all relatives including children. Here the distinction made a difference. When relatives were defined as kin other than offspring, there was no effect of additional children for loans made. Additional children, that is, do not lead to a reduction in loans to other relatives. When relatives were defined to include children, however, the negative effect shown in Figure 6.5 emerged. The reduction in loans, therefore, appears to be to children, which means that the changing composition of the married couple household (i.e., number of children) matters less than who is included as a relative. As children are the primary recipients of both gifts and loans from parents, we can make sense of the findings. The normative dimensions of marriage appear to matter in the expected way for gifts and loans to relatives so long as we are talking about relatives *other than children*. However, as households grow to include more children, less is loaned to each offspring, even though loans to *other relatives* are unaffected.

Married men (couples) appear to allocate their gifts and loans to relatives in ways that agree with the model of normative marriage. They do not, however, treat their *own children* the way they treat other relatives. All measures of gifts and loans refer to those made to people who do not live in the household. If parents treat their children more or less equally, then more children in the household would probably lead to lower levels of transfers to those no longer living at home (in college, or elsewhere). One cannot know if this is the actual reason for the findings, but it is entirely consistent with them.

With this as a possible explanation for the negative effect of additional children for loans to relatives, attention should focus on the broad consistency between how gifts and loans are affected by marriage and changes in it. When one considers loans to nonrelatives, the most significant departures from all previous findings appear. Two dimensions of marriage affect such loans (maturity and parenthood). The greater the level of family financial independence, the *lower* the amount of loans to nonrelatives. Likewise, the addition of children to the married household also *reduces* such loans. This, of course, accords with earlier findings that showed transitions into marriage associated with reductions in this type of loan in the early years, whereas transitions out of marriage had the opposite effect. Now it becomes possible to understand those patterns. The pooling of resources and earnings in a marriage probably leads to greater financial independence than is found among recently widowed or divorced men. And, marriage produces children. Both financial independence and the presence of children reduce loans to nonfamily members in amounts comparable to those found for the transitions into and out of marriage, as seen in Figure 6.6.

The results have shown that men in increasingly normative marriages make greater gifts and loans to their relatives. But a qualification should be added to this finding—children are not treated the same as other relatives. Parents appear to treat children more equally. The more children there are, the less any one receives.

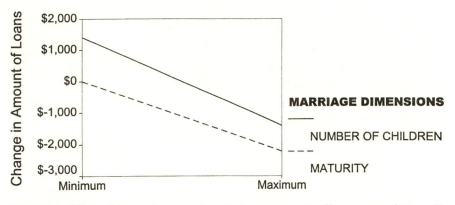

Figure 6.6. *Effects of changes in normative marriage on amounts of loans to nonrelatives.* All values are in constant 1993 dollars. Data from the National Survey of Families and Households: 1987–1994.

The situation for nonfamily members is the opposite. At least with respect to loans, in increasingly normative marriages less money flows to such people. Quite simply, marriage, especially normative marriage, leads to greater generosity to relatives and less to others.

What Does Generosity Mean?

The analysis of gifts and loans shows that they are affected by changes in men's marriages in much the same way achievement and personal communities are. As men's marriages become more normative, they give more money to relatives, exactly as one would have predicted. But what are we to make of people other than family? Why does marriage reduce gifts and loans to such people?

Some of the reductions in this type of exchange are unrelated to the degree of traditionalism in a man's marriage. Gifts to people who are not relatives drop shortly after marriage, but they were not responsive to changes in normative dimensions of marriage. Clearly, something about marriage matters (at least in the earliest years) in relation to gifts. These analyses do not specify that something.

Still, there is enough consistency to the pattern of results to conclude that people who are not part of the kinship group become less compelling as recipients once a man gets married. And as the last chapter showed, such people are less likely to be part of men's personal communities. That research also showed that marriage reduces contacts with friends and casual associates. The findings about gifts and loans, therefore, are more understandable when we realize that married men spend less time with friends than they did before they married. Remember also that married men spend *more* time with relatives than they did before marriage. The changes found for exchanges of money mirror exactly those found for personal communities. Marriage, especially very normative marriage, shifts a man's orientation from friends to relatives, as it does from informal to role-based relationships.

When a man buys a birthday gift for his niece, or his wife's brother, he is doing something scripted in our institution of marriage. He is conforming to custom, but he is doing much more. His gift is something he does as part of his role as a member of the kinship network, something married men do for their relatives as a part of what it means to be a husband.

There are no comparable expectations concerning nonfamily members. Absent any strong system of expectations that a man give to such individuals, he is less likely to do so. As the evidence makes clear, he typically doesn't. In the exchange of gifts, just as in the construction of personal communities, married men stress the kinship because relations with relatives are strongly governed by rules, whereas relationships with most people are not.

The dimensions of marriage that influence gifts and loans generally have consistent effects. More traditional (normative) marriages are typically associated with greater transfers to relatives. The dimensions of maturity, free choice, and fidelity operated in just this way. Children, however, can and do have the opposite consequences. However, just as in men's personal communities, children have this effect because men's primary obligations appear to be to their own children first. And the same factors that lead to greater transfers to relatives also lead to smaller transfers to other people. In this, as with personal communities, men appear to reallocate their gifts and loans rather than make significant absolute changes. Indeed, the aggregate (total) amount of gifts and loans does not change nearly so much as the configuration of recipients.

Does this mean that gifts are nothing more than a way of discharging the obligations of kinship for men? Perhaps. But it is also entirely possible that they have the meanings I discussed earlier in this chapter. Giving to his relatives probably does make a man *feel good*. By his gifts he affirms his ability to give. One cannot easily help others if one is needy. To give to others requires a certain amount of economic independence. It is not surprising, therefore, that family independence fostered greater giving to relatives. Giving probably reinforces a man's sense of his independence and ability. To give is to display and also to experience these traits oneself. In these ways, the gifts a married man makes sustain his masculinity.

NOTES

1. The question wording changed slightly between waves. In the first wave, respondents were asked to report on the amount of gifts (over $200) they had made to each of the categories listed. In the second wave, they were asked to report on the largest *two* gifts because fewer than 1% of respondents reported more than two such gifts in Wave 1. In analyses reported in this chapter, I have structured the Time 1 data to conform with the Time 2

format in the following way: for each question asked (gifts and loans), I selected the two *largest* reports and discarded any others. This made the data comparable across waves. The difference in the value of money (across waves) was also considered by adjusting all dollars to Time 2 values according to the change in overall CPI. This adjustment had no discernible effect on the pattern of findings, even while changing the magnitude of coefficients. The values reported in Appendix C and the figures in this chapter are in 1993 dollars (i.e., Time 1 values were inflated to Time 2 values).

2. The fact that the large majority of men gave nothing to each category of kin studied meant that the methods of analysis (regression) used in earlier chapters were inappropriate. The problem in these data is censoring. Large percentages of cases have no values for gifts given, whereas a small percentage do. Among those who do have a value entered, the range is actually quite large. Such left-censored data require alternative methods of estimation to avoid bias. Tobit estimators were used for all equations estimated in this chapter. This procedure works by first estimating a PROBIT model of which respondents have data and which don't (i.e., which did and which did not make gifts or loans). A function of the probit is then included as a regressor in an OLS (see, Heckman, 1976), or maximum likelihood solution. The latter approach was followed in this work, using the TOBIT routine in statistical package STATA.

✦ 7 ✦

The New Normative Marriage

Is It Good for Men?

By binding himself to the social institution of marriage, a man builds and sustains himself in predictable ways. Marriage changes men by improving their accomplishments. *Marriage in Men's Lives* shows that the soft boundaries surrounding private married life provide a template for activities in public life as well. Married men are more involved than unmarried men in the impersonal and rational world of work, where the rewards are public and measured in dollars or prestige. There are clear models, or standards, to follow in such pursuits, and success (or failure) is easily recognized. Married men alter their personal communities by shifting allegiance from informal or personal friendships to relationships in patterned and normative roles, where performance is easily judged by conformity to accepted principles. And married men change their model of help and assistance to conform with expectations about socially accepted standards of responsibility and obligations, especially to relatives. In these ways, and perhaps many others, marriage structures men's lives around standards and rules that are known and appreciated in our society.

Husbands organize much of their life in accordance with expectations of them *as husbands*. Married men structure their lives by reference to social position and hierarchy. They stress social roles that are components of public institutions (in the economy and religion, for example). The traits expected of married men as husbands are those expected of husbands as men: responsibility (for wife and children), maturity, and fidelity. Marriage may be the venue for the expression and maintenance of masculinity, but it is also a metaphor for much more in men's lives. Married men are more productive and less dependent than unmarried men. Marriage fosters a type of engagement with others in which the husband is an active, independent provider who lives in a world of objective and often impersonal rules. This is part of the basic script for what it means to be an American man. It is the antithesis of femininity, from a man's perspective. The relationships that married men establish and become involved in are not *created* so much as they are entered or joined. They do not require that a man develop a relationship so much as they require that he become a member or conform to a model of one.

Men are judged, and probably judge themselves, as "good" or "bad" husbands (and fathers). They can do this because the standards are shared and known. They inhere in the definition of normative marriage. *Good* husbands are mature, faithful, generous fathers and providers. Good husbands are good men. Success as a husband, like success in other areas of men's lives, is measured in conventional ways. One can recognize the good (or bad) provider, the faithful father, or the mature husband. Indeed, the standards by which husbands are judged (and probably judge themselves) are quite well-known, at least for the present, because there are so few other options in men's lives. Similarly, the ways a man can be a good husband are quite restricted. Socially and culturally, at least, the model of matrimony has remained fairly constant and rigid for men, even though it may have changed for women.

The husband who, with his wife, constructs a new model of marriage faces significant challenges. The man who is the primary homemaker or child-care provider, or whose wife is the sole wage earner, will probably find such novel arrangements difficult, but not impossible, to sustain. Relations with parents may become awkward. Friends may find it difficult to understand and appreciate the arrangement, especially if it departs from their own. And employers may respond in the same way. As I have shown, such men's private lives (as husbands to their wives) and also their public lives will differ. They will probably work fewer hours and earn less. They will be less involved in public community organizations, less likely to belong to or attend church, and less embedded in extensive networks of exchange and help with relatives. Certainly some men are able to organize their lives this way, but they face challenges that originate not at home but in all the other social institutions. Every social institution embodies presumptions about gender. Since normative marriage is the basis of prevailing assumptions about husbands, such men will be viewed as deviating from convention. If men deviate in significant and obvious ways from the prevailing institutional assumptions about marriage, they will probably pay a price. But, clearly, growing numbers of men must pay such a price, and many appear willing to.

The Problems with Normative Marriage

A different model of marriage is emerging, as it must, in response to significant changes in women's lives. The title of a recent book on the future of American families posed the stark question: *New Families, or No Families?* Its authors say, "New families are being formed, in which men and women share family economic responsibilities as well as the domestic tasks that ensure that family members go to work or school clean, clothed, fed, and rested, and come home to a place where they provide each other care and comfort" (Goldscheider and Waite, 1991: xiii).

If this is true, women will find it increasingly difficult to define themselves as lifetime homemakers, even for those few who might wish to. Increases in life expectancy, declines in fertility, and the growing instability of marriages (i.e., divorce) make such an option quite problematic for women because it leaves them with few options after children leave home or their marriages end. Increasingly, wives are sharing with husbands the tasks of providing for the family and maintaining it. In some ways, the trend toward greater sharing of economic responsibilities and household maintenance is a return to an older pattern. Rural wives in the nineteenth century were integral parts of their family economies. Similarly, urban wives took in boarders or lodgers, did other families' laundry, or performed other remunerated services in their homes (Cherlin,1996: 479). We often forget that the family with a full-time homemaker wife not counted on to make a direct contribution to the household economy was a late-nineteenth- and early-twentieth-century transitory pattern (Coontz, 1992).

There is little reason to believe that Americans will suddenly rediscover and embrace this "traditional" marriage pattern (husband as sole earner, wife as homemaker). Nor is there any reason to think that recent changes in women's lives bring no consequence for marriages, families, and husbands. The emergence of "new families" is a well-documented fact, even if we have not fully come to terms with it (Spain and Bianchi, 1996).

The challenge that "modern" or "new" marriage presents to men, therefore, is how to reconcile private and public lives. How will men successfully integrate the new aspects of intimate family life with their engagement with, or membership in, public social roles? Before answering this, I ask you to consider the model of normative marriage one final time. What is the relationship between spouses in such traditional marriages? When married men conform to the model of traditional marriage, they are fathers, providers, and protectors—the universal trinity of roles that define adult men. Such men have not been, however, on purely equal footing with their wives. On certain core dimensions, there is inequality. In fact, normative marriage is a complex system of interdependencies (or inequalities). And inequalities based on sex are the aspect of normative marriage now being challenged most forcefully. How will men accommodate greater equality in their marriages?

Marriages will surely continue to become even more equal partnerships. But if some amount of differentiation (or inequality) in marriage contributes to what it means to "be" a husband, and if it is also part of what it means to conform to cultural ideals of masculinity, then what will greater equality imply? Now we are broaching the core of traditional American marriage; complex inequalities exist in who does what and who is responsible for whom, inequalities based on sex.

In the past few decades, Americans have witnessed a profound redefinition of one element of marriage—what it means to be a married woman. Wives are now typically employed and share more equally the tasks of providing for the family. Fertility has declined, and marriage is entered into later in life when men and women are farther along their chosen career paths. All such changes have undoubtedly been challenging (even if rewarding) to women because there has not been a clear model of how to incorporate them into a marriage. Women who marry today will probably create marriages that depart significantly from those of their grandmothers. But even though women's lives have changed and the options available have expanded, the basic dimensions of marriage remain pretty much the same as they have been for decades. The change in gender has focused on women's lives in almost every way except their marriages—that is, the revolution in women's lives has not extended to marriage for either women *or* men.

Men who marry today are part of these changes, to be sure. But how are men to reconcile the new model of womanhood within the normative model of marriage that is central to their masculinity? The answer is that we must now focus on what it means to be a husband and hold men to different standards than their fathers were. Yet this new model of normative marriage will not be a wholesale departure from contemporary patterns, even if it is experienced very differently by married spouses.

The gender inequality that is part of the traditional institution of marriage is, by most accounts, the "problem." So it is important to consider the nature and meaning of it. Although many types of inequality (especially relative power) are experienced as unfair, some are the foundation for enduring and satisfying partnerships. The union of two persons with differing talents, resources, or abilities may produce a sum much greater than its parts. To the extent that husbands and wives are not completely equal partners in all ways, some amount of enforced dependency is built into the marriage. For instance, consider income. When husbands are the sole providers, wives depend on that income in ways they would not if each spouse earned equally. If she does the housework and child care, he may depend on her for such services. These patterns are well-known and often translate into feelings of inequity for one or both partners. However, not all types of inequalities produce such undesirable consequences.

Some types of inequality in marriage are better described as enforced dependencies, that is, depending on something from your partner that you could not realistically provide for yourself. Normative marriage in its present form results in greater dependencies than can be expected in more equal, sharing, and "modern" marriages. As marriage is redefined to be a more egalitarian partnership, one consequence is lower levels of enforced dependencies. Completely equal partners will depend less on one another. At some point, however, the independence born of complete equality has the potential to weaken the solidarity of marriages. After all, two excellent soloists do not make a very good duet.

Couples who depend heavily on one another for many things, including income and household tasks, are more committed to their marriages. Both husbands and wives in such relationships perceive greater negative consequences for ending their unions than those who are less dependent on one another. Moreover, the *perception* of dependence is very strongly related to commitment in marriage. Spouses who believe that their partners depend on them are themselves more committed to maintaining the marriage (Nock, 1995).

Research on divorce has made this point repeatedly. To the extent that enforced dependency is responsible for marital stability, most believe that women's economic independence (through involvement in the paid labor force) *allows* wives to leave abusive or loveless marriages or to forego marriage altogether. For this reason, the increase in divorce rates since 1960 is typically attributed to the growing participation of married women in the paid labor force (Cherlin, 1992).

The findings reported in this book might be taken to imply that men cannot easily have egalitarian marriages while still "doing gender." But that is not the message I hope to convey. It may be that certain dependencies in marriage are central to men's sense of themselves as effective adult males. Few women or men object to dependency per se. Rather, it is the nature of such dependencies that is the problem, especially the extent to which they are perceived or experienced as inequitable, unfair, or excessively restrictive.

The New Normative Marriage

In intimate relationships, inequity is a subjective assessment about the nature of enforced dependency. It is possible to envision a restructuring of marriage that eliminates the basic causes of inequity without eliminating all dependencies. In fact, such a model of marriage is quite possible even if we have not yet, as a society, pursued such a strategy openly. Instead, the fundamental gender changes we know so well have been quite one-sided because the inequities have been so one-sided. Major social change has focused on wives and women, not on men. And, most important, such changes have not focused on marriages. We appear to be pursuing gender equality in all areas as a remedy for the well-known inequities women have suffered except in their marriages. In the pursuit of such equality, it is important to consider how it will "fit" within marriages.

It *will* fit, but only in a new institution of marriage founded on extensive dependencies that are not inherently inequitable. There is probably a good explanation for why this idea has not attracted much consideration; such a model of marriage would require that men depend on women as often as women depend on men. Clearly, if a new and equitable model of marriage is to be forged, it must focus on males, in their roles as husbands and men and dependents.

However, other alternatives to traditional normative marriage can be imagined. Few are realistic for most people. One is a form of the family that omits an adult pair—a single-parent family. Despite much attention devoted to the growth of such arrangements, they are not an alternative to normative marriage for many. The very affluent who can support themselves and their children on one income may be able to sustain such a family arrangement. And the very poor who rely on government assistance (Medicaid, welfare, subsidized housing, food stamps) may also be able to live in such families, at least for a short time. But very few single parents in America will be able to satisfy the needs of their families on their own.

One should not confuse the prevalence of single-parent families with the potential for such families to replace more traditional (husband/wife) arrangements. Indeed, the chronic problems faced by unmarried parents and their children are significant and pervasive. Single parents do not have the resources to support their own households in most cases, nor do they have the time or energy. Children in such families receive less parental contact than those in two-parent families. They move frequently, disrupting schooling, friends, and the parent's social networks. In the end, such children typically finish fewer years of school, and are more likely to drop out of school, and are more likely to have children outside of marriage, receive welfare, and become involved in undesirable behaviors (McLanahan and Sandefur, 1994). Unless other sources of support (economic, housing, day care, etc.) become available in significant amounts in the future, such a family structure is unworkable as a normative institution. As recent trends in welfare legislation make clear, we are unwilling, as a nation, to increase the level of public support for these types of families.

Another alternative is a new model of marriage disconnected from masculine identity. Might it be possible to redefine manhood in such a way that traditional normative marriage is not central? In fact, I believe this is highly unlikely, if not impossible. The very close association between marriage and adult masculinity is universal and has withstood many challenges, as we have seen in earlier chapters. So if we are unlikely to redefine masculinity as separate (or separable) from marriage, or to redefine the family as headed by a single adult, the best alternative is to redefine marriage to be consistent with husband's lives as men, but also with women's lives as equal partners. Is it possible to define normative marriage to be equitable while still offering men the opportunity to be fathers, providers, and protectors? This, it seems to me, is the real challenge.

The source of inequity in marriage is not gender inequality (i.e., gender dependency) per se. Rather, it is the nature of such inequalities, especially the one-sided character of them. Nor is the source of inequity normative marriage or its close association with masculinity. The inequity in traditional marriage is the *coercive* and unilateral nature of so many enforced dependencies, the fact that women have had so little choice and so little power. An equitable marriage is one in which both spouses are voluntarily bound by the dependencies that are the basis of their commitment. Freely chosen dependency in marriage is the desirable goal, not complete equality in all matters. Such dependencies need not jeopardize women's (or men's) present or future opportunities. A complex division of responsibilities and tasks is the practical basis for unity in marriage. Without extensive dependencies, the only thing that unites two spouses is affection or love. But love and affection alone are flimsy bases for enduring marriages unless supported by other types of bonds. Cohabiting relationships, for example, lack such pervasive links. Such partnerships endure, or fail, solely as a result of the persistence of affectionate bonds. Small wonder that such partnerships do not endure for long. Something else is needed. And that something else is the institutional and normative outline that casts husbands and wives in *mutually* dependent roles.

What is the difference between complete equality and freely chosen dependency? In some cases, nothing except a way of seeing things differently. The two spouses who actually earn equal incomes are certainly capable of recognizing their mutual dependence on their combined income. But so are spouses who have very different incomes, even if one has none for a period of time. Institutions are not subject to legislation or significant intentional change in the short run. Rather, institutions change as customary beliefs about them change. The new model of marriage beginning to emerge is the consequence of slow changes in such beliefs and presumptions.

To ask if we can have equitable normative marriage is to ask about the content of the institution. This question can be stated in terms of the core dimensions of the institution. Can marriages based on free choice be fair to women? Is the presumption of maturity compatible with a sense that the relationship is equitable? Do the ideas of monogamy and fidelity preclude a fair partnership? Is there something inherently inequitable about heterosexual unions? And do children necessarily cast wives in inflexible and unfair positions? In fact, there is little about any of these marriage norms that is *necessarily* problematic. And that leads to a final question. What about the idea that husbands should be the heads of their households?

This dimension of marriage has been studied by focusing on relative incomes, and I will use that as an illustration of my basic point. If one defines marriage as a relationship that presumes greater earnings by husbands, then there will probably be inequity because economic dominance often translates into other forms. Yet this dimension of marriage need not carry invidious implications. Historically, of course, it has. And husbands' economic roles in families often translated into their roles as sole representatives of the family to the larger community and the public.

The question, then, is how to cast men in their roles as providers (and protectors) when wives earn some or most of the family income? This is not difficult to imagine. The normative expectation for married men is that they provide for their wives and children. Alternatively, this means that wives and children are their dependents. It is not necessarily the case (now or in the past) that husbands must do *all* the providing, however. It is only that men must be (i.e., it is normative to be) engaged in such pursuits. A new model of marriage will retain this basic presumption by requiring that men work, not that they necessarily earn more than their wives. Such a pattern is quickly emerging. In 1995, almost all (95%) married men with children in the household were employed. Almost two-thirds (65%) of wives in such families were employed. Husbands (especially those with children) are expected to work. The expectations for women are not so rigid, yet more and more wives are earning incomes (U. S. Bureau of the Census, 1996a: Table 15).

This does not eliminate the wife's dependence on her husband. It does, however, mean that more and more husbands are also dependents. Spouses can be heavily dependent on one another's income, even while both earn significant amounts. A married lifestyle is built on the combined resources generated by the spouses. When this lifestyle depends on the continued earnings of both husband and wife, there is mutual dependency like that probably found in nineteenth century rural families (and many contemporary marriages as well). And this, it would seem, is a very modest redefinition of normative marriage. New marriages will still require that husbands provide for their wives (and children). The shift is that husbands *and* wives come to see themselves as dependents in an ongoing cooperative enterprise. Dependency, that is, must become equalized.

This does not mean that husbands must become more dependent on their wives so much as it means that husbands must reconcile that dependency with the assumption of corresponding responsibilities. Even if most married couples today depend on one another's earnings, traditional patterns of domestic responsibilites persist. Many of the problems mentioned by married and divorced couples coalesce around this main issue. Even when wives are employed for pay, husbands do not yet appear willing to share equitably the responsibilities for child care and household tasks (Hochschild and Machung, 1989). Dependency in such matters, that is, is not yet equalized. Housework, as noted earlier, is part of "doing gender." Husbands appear unwilling to assume greater responsibilities for tasks culturally defined as women's. Because the household is the venue for the display of gender, such reluctance is, perhaps, understandable. At the same time, cultural definitions of what it means to be a woman and a wife are changing, as indicated by the widespread involvement of married women in paid labor. To repeat an earlier point, we must now focus on what it means to be a husband and a married man. If we do not, then the mutual economic dependence so common today will simply translate into more work for wives and the problems this creates (e.g., divorce). Perhaps the legacy of a traditional division of tasks has been supported by the greater relative earnings of husbands. One reason to believe that the type of changes I am describing may occur is that there is growing equality between husbands' and wives' earnings. Increasingly, spouses are in marriages wherein the relative earnings of the two partners are closer, if not equal (Spain and Bianchi, 1996).

The evidence I have presented shows that relative earnings *do* matter. When mens' incomes exceed those of their wives, there were large and predictable consequences. But does this imply that husbands must be sole or primary providers? Probably not, if historical patterns are any guide. Even if contemporary marriages are now based on such assumptions, there is no necessary reason to believe that this one core dimension might not be altered with very positive general consequences. As the earnings gap between husbands and wives has narrowed among younger cohorts, there has been a small increase in the amount of housework that husbands do (Spain and Bianchi, 1996). Things are changing, as they must.

In short, a new model of marriage is already emerging. Legally, at least, marriage is much less gendered than it was two or three decades ago. Still, marriage and the family are, and will remain, an important locale for "doing gender," especially for men. The changes we are likely to see in the institution of marriage do *not* portend the end of gender in marriage. They do, hopefully, mean the end of invidious inequalities based on gender in marriage.

Few boys today will grow up with mothers who are not employed. Fewer young men will inherit their father's or grandfather's traditional views about marriage or women. Fewer men work with colleagues who openly view women and wives in traditional restricted roles. More and more of the youthful life course is spent in nontraditional families or outside of families altogether. Children, especially boys, who experience such childhoods (employed mothers, divorce, nonfamily living) are more accepting of women's new roles and options and willing to perform more housework (Goldscheider and Waite, 1991). It is not, therefore, a dramatic change in the basic institution of normative marriage that we are now beginning to see. Rather, it is a recognition and accommodation to changes in gender. Even if this is not a fundamental redefinition of marriage, it will have profound consequences for how women experience marriages.

The new model of normative marriage will be good for men (just as the prevailing model is) if it is founded on freely accepted interdependencies. But the new model of marriage that is emerging will be better for women than the one I have been describing in this book. In fact, *contemporary* marriages are good for women, even though there are significant flaws. They just aren't as good for women as they are for men.

A book about marriage in men's lives implicitly asks how the sexes differ. In fact, marriage has many of the same consequences for women and men, but for very different reasons. I replicated all analyses presented in the last three chapters on the women in the samples. First, I made comparisons of women before and after they married. Then I made comparisons among married women using the same dimensions of normative marriage studied for men. The first set of results revealed similar types of consequences of marriage for both sexes, though consistently much smaller for women (slight increases in annual incomes and occupational prestige, modest shifts in personal communities, and increases in transfers to relatives). The second set of results showed, however, that the reasons for those effects are not the same for husbands and wives. Indeed, few dimensions of normative marriage had the same types of consequences for women that they had for men, but this should not be surprising. One of the guiding assumptions of this work is that men change as a result of being married (i.e., the role of being a husband), whereas women are more likely to respond to the *quality* of the relationship. We do not really know why marriage changes women, but the simple fact that the changes following marriage are similar for the two sexes raises some very provocative questions. As I noted at the outset of this book, there are two marriages in every marital union. Even if "his" marriage is better than "hers," both partners are changed by it (probably for the better). The question about women is the same as it is for men. Why?

Historically, women were even more restricted in their adult options than men were. While marriage may have been the typical route to adult status for men, it was more than that for women because there were so few opportunities for female self-support. That is certainly less true today, although marriage is still a major factor in women's economic circumstances. Economic factors are probably not adequate to explain fully the effects of marriage for women, but our study of men may offer some guidance.

Marriage may be part of wives' identities as women. If the family is the arena for the expression and development of male gender, then it is difficult to imagine that it does so only for men. How marriage contributes to femininity, of course, is obviously quite different from the way it contributes to masculinity. Women's family lives have been dominated by their responsibilities for caring for children, homemaking, and maintaining kinship connections. Perhaps such structured responsibilities in domestic life contributed in some way to wives' feminine identities. Perhaps the unmarried woman, the "spinster" or "old maid," is viewed as less feminine than her married counterpart. We do not know, and we need to investigate how and why marriage changes women.

There are many challenges to marriage in our times. Most of them have two common sources. For one, greater independence (economic and otherwise) has eroded some of the reasons to marry or remain married. Love and affection are increasingly the only glue that binds couples together. When love fades, as it often does for short or long periods in intimate relationships, then other facets must exist to maintain the stability of a marriage. And there are simply fewer alternative bonds today. The other, related challenge is more directly connected to the profound changes in women's lives in the past 50 years. What it now means to be a wife is very different from what it meant in prior generations. Neither women nor men have fully adjusted to these changes in their private married lives, although public life is much less confusing.

We should see these challenges as the source of institutional change. Marriage is now being redefined because traditional assumptions are no longer valid. And many of those assumptions pertain to the meaning of gender. These are not new issues. Indeed, we have confronted these very same issues in other social institutions. In law, business, education, politics, and religion, the gender battles have been waged openly in public. And these institutions are different today than they were before such challenges were made. The family is the last basic social institution to be confronted by these fundamental issues of what it means to be a man or a woman. Change in the family institution is slower and more difficult than in the other realms of society because the issues associated with them are typically confronted in private. Individuals who struggle in their own marriages see their problems as personal, just as they see the solutions. But, cumulatively, these individual troubles coalesce and produce large social change by becoming defined as legitimate public issues.

We are not going to see the end of marriage any time soon. Nor are we going to see the end of gender. The close connection between these two aspects of adult identity and social organization is the central message of this book. In a very basic sense, real men are still husbands. Even as we recognize the growing diversity in living arrangements, traditional marriage is still the way most men and women will share intimacies and raise their children. Husbands will still work to provide for their wives and children. Husbands will benefit from the presumptions of maturity, heterosexuality, and independence associated with being married. Men will still marry with the expectation that their unions will last. And husbands will be changed by their marriages. They will earn and achieve more. They will become members of organizations devoted to improving communities. They will be generous to their relatives. These are things our society values. Those who engage in them earn our respect and thanks. Collectively, we value and depend on such people. When men marry, they are more likely to make such contributions. They become better men.

APPENDICES

Appendix A

Multivariate Results for Chapter 4

Pooled Cross-Section Time-Series with Fixed Effects

Table A.1. *Changes in Marital Status*

Variable	B	S.E.	Sig.	Average[a]
	A. Changes in Weeks Worked[b]			
Age	1.143	0.015	.000	0.575
Married	2.232	0.178	.000	0.019
Divorced	−1.085	0.362	.003	0.005
Widowed	−7.418	2.049	.000	0.000
Remarried	−3.020	0.525	.000	0.002
	B. Changes in Occupational Prestige[c]			
Age	0.782	0.019	.000	1.024
Married	1.763	0.213	.000	0.042
Divorced	−1.371	0.427	.001	0.008
Widowed	−2.471	2.459	.315	0.000
Remarried	−1.301	0.608	.032	0.003
	C. Changes in Annual Income[d]			
Age	1495.85	28.91	.000	0.517
Married	4260.85	332.14	.000	0.019
Divorced	90.10	675.67	.894	0.005
Widowed	−2645.49	3812.06	.487	0.000
Remarried	−2745.72	978.25	.005	0.002

Note: No constant. Regression through the origin for fixed-effects analyses

[a] Mean deviation from personal mean

[b] $N = 68,361$ person years $R^2 = .119$ ($F = 1850.98$, sig = .000)

[c] $N = 52,987$ person years $R^2 = .053$ ($F = 597.58$, sig = .000)

[d] $N = 68,418$ person years $R^2 = .068$ ($F = 1008.27.58$, sig =.000)

Table A.2. *Changes in Marriage Dimensions*

Variable	B	S.E.	Sig.	Average[a]
	A. Weeks Worked[b]			
Age[c]	0.750	0.034	.000	−.001
Sex ratio	5.723	0.355	.000	.053
Spouse dependency	8.852	0.236	.000	−.001
Family independence	16.402	0.437	.000	.008
No children[d]	−2.112	0.276	.000	−.204
No. of children[e]	0.056	0.156	.722	.410
Yrs. married	0.920	0.035	.000	1.612
	B. Occupational Prestige[f]			
Age	0.959	.049	.000	.027
Sex ratio	2.889	.503	.000	.055
Spouse dependency	0.109	.503	.000	.013
Family independence	1.257	.649	.052	.011
No children[d]	−1.590	.397	.000	−.213
No. of children[e]	−0.513	.222	.021	.423
Yrs. married	0.963	.050	.000	1.647
	C. Annual Income[g]			
Age	1592.91	89.38	.000	.001
Sex ratio	3201.96	921.78	.000	.053
Spouse dependency	10222.37	612.34	.000	.001
Family independence	33314.57	1132.95	.000	.008
No children[d]	−1705.08	714.45	.000	−.204
No. of children[e]	−6.67	405.41	.987	.410
Yrs. married	1826.38	90.81	.000	1.612

Note: No constant. Regression through the origin for fixed-effects analyses

[a] Mean deviation from personal mean

[b] $N = 18,333$ person years $R^2 = .276$ ($F = 1000.28$, sig = .000)

[c] Age is represented throughout as the residual of age regressed on other age-related variables in the equation (age-specific sex ratio, years married).

[d] 1 = none, 0 = some

[e] That is, the actual number of children greater than 0 (1, 2, 3, etc.)

[f] $N = 16,456$ person years $R^2 = .071$ ($F = 178.41$, sig = .000)

[g] $N = 18,336$ person years $R^2 = .134$ ($F = 404.39$, sig = .000)

Appendix B

Multivariate Results for Chapter 5

Conditional Change Models

Table B.1. *Effects of Marital Status on Social Interaction*

	Dependent Variables							
Independent Variable	Relatives	Neighbors	Co-workers	Friends	Church Social Events	Church Services	Bar/Tavern	Group Recreation
	Time 2							
First marriage	.176*	.031	.129*	−.290*	.206*	.331*	−.379*	−.069
Divorced	−.162*	−.007	.121*	.116	−.104	−.244*	.251*	.046
Widowed	−.058	.439*	.345*	−.207	.087	−.167	−.193	−.192
Remarried	.127	.108	.022	−.160	.043	.177	−.199*	−.049
	Time 1							
First marriage	.008	−.064	−.142*	.264*	.162*	.295*	−.223*	−.037
Divorced	.060	−.065	−.064	−.063	.140*	.169*	−.104	−.069
Widowed	−.162	−.166	−.202	.048	.175	.845*	−.219	−.180
Remarried	−.138*	−.022	−.160	.043	.177	.255*	−.194*	−.045
Age	.018	.003	.026	−.009	.028*	.015	.003	−.056*
Dependent variable at time 1	.308*	.168*	.160*	.176*	.301*	.573*	.343*	.326*
Constant	.090	.039	.059	.076	.127	−.010	.096	.420
R^2	.093*	.039*	.059*	.076*	.127*	.353*	.181*	.120*
N	3,373	3,290	3,336	3,390	3,604	3,604	3,372	3,431

Notes: Conditional Change Models estimated with OLS regression.
Coefficients shown are metric regression coefficients.
All dependent variables are represented as z-scores.
* $p < .05$

Table B.2. *Effects of Marital Status on Participation in Organizations*

Independent Variable	Dependent Variables			
	Church Group	Service Organization	Work Group	Sport Hobby
	Time 2			
First marriage	2.486*	0.783*	0.681*	0.552
Divorced	0.934	0.981	1.104	1.094
Widowed	1.266	0.359*	0.644	0.653
Remarried	1.519	1.315	0.984	0.658
	Time 1			
First marriage	1.529*	1.019	1.116	0.994
Divorced	0.967	0.837	0.877	0.992
Widowed	1.073	0.198*	0.806	1.070
Remarried	1.254	0.993	1.032	1.178
Age	1.007	1.018*	1.011*	0.980*
Dependent variable at time 1	6.612*	4.454*	4.285*	3.209*
-2ll change (over base model)	789.9*	514.2*	561.4*	397.1*
N	2,953	2,972	2,425	2,951

Notes: Conditional Change Models estimated with logistic regression.

Coefficients shown are changes in odds (exponentiated logistic regression coefficient).

* p < .05

Table B.3. *Effects of Marriage Dimensions on Social Interaction*

					Dependent Variables			
Independent Variable	Relatives	Neighbors	Coworkers	Friends	Church Social Events	Church Services	Bar/Tavern	Group Recreation
					Time 2			
Sex ratio	.037	-.336	-.274	-.148	.048	.429	-.189	-.054
Family independence	-.238*	-.079	.179*	.036	.052	.072	-.071	-.101
Spouse dependency	.052	.079*	.030	-.050	-.039	.112*	-.076*	-.046
No. of children	.022	-.030	-.084*	-.042*	.102*	.125*	-.040*	-.062*
Yrs. married	.009*	-.022	-.008	-.012	-.009	-.003	.007*	.016
					Time 1			
Sex ratio	-.237	.319	.344	-.204	-.008	.074	.078	.295
Family independence	-.016	-.012	-.016	.145	-.084	-.118	.093	.022
Spouse dependency	-.027	-.037	.053	-.017	-.049	-.105*	.022	.056
No. of children	-.066	-.010	.026	-.013	-.016	-.012	.036	.013
Yrs. married	.018	.028	.006	-.018	.007	.002	.001	-.010
Age[a]	-.003	.002	-.001	-.010	.006	.019	-.016*	-.015
Dependent variable at time 1	.376*	.243*	.233*	.225*	.337*	.626*	.447*	.405*
Constant	.835	.121	-.212	.777	-.610	-1.270	.366	.681
R^2	.163*	.064*	.071*	.078*	.160*	.412*	.250*	.194*
N	1,545	1,532	1,538	1,549	1,567	1,636	1,560	1,580

Notes: Conditional Change Models estimated with OLS regression.
Coefficients shown are metric regression coefficients.
All dependent variables are represented as z-scores.
[a] Age is represented as the residual of age regressed on other age-related variables in the equation (age-specific sex ratio, years married).
* $p < .05$

Table B.4. *Effects of Marriage Dimensions on Participation in Organizations*

Independent Variable	Church Group	Service Organization	Work Group	Sport Hobby
		Dependent Variables		
	Time 2			
Sex ratio	1.000	0.474	0.323*	0.538
Family independence	2.005*	1.417	2.023*	0.852
Spouse dependency	0.974	0.866*	1.361*	0.913
No. of children	1.126	1.043	0.954	0.981
Yrs. married	0.979	0.995	0.978*	0.933
	Time 1			
Sex ratio	0.350*	2.179	1.005	0.481
Family independence	1.182	2.497*	1.326	0.802
Spouse dependency	0.856	1.085	0.960	0.922
No. of children	1.042	0.869*	1.083	1.052
Yrs. married	1.001	1.013	1.007	1.067
Age[a]	1.013	0.998	0.996	1.021
Dependent variable at time 1	8.536*	3.076*	5.510*	4.553*
2ll change	423.6*	141.8*	292.1*	188.1*
N	1,355	1,354	1,363	1,366

Notes: Conditional Change Models estimated with logistic regression.

Coefficients shown are changes in odds (exponentiated logistic regression coefficient).

[a] Age is the residual of age regressed on other age-related variables in the equation.

* $p < .05$

Appendix C

Multivariate Results for Chapter 6

Conditional Change Models

Table C.1. *Effects of Marital Status on Giving and Loaning*

Independent Variable	Dependent Variables			
	Gifts to Relatives	Gifts to Nonrelatives	Loans to Relatives	Loans to Nonrelatives
Time 2				
First marriage	−717.39	−1874.74*	2603.47*	−2296.01*
Divorced	530.36	1275.54*	−812.82	1949.70*
Widowed	182.95	538.39	−162.66	3881.07*
Remarried	432.63	−1050.26*	1570.61	−2073.40*
Time 1				
First marriage	369.55	−1730.58*	1991.26*	−1732.74*
Divorced	−481.78	−934.86*	2379.40*	261.36
Widowed	-3434.83	153.63	973.01	−1733.01
Remarried	24.59	−1235.62*	852.87	−985.87
Age	176.92*	−42.76*	94.06*	−23.25
Dependent variable at time 1	.277*	.118*	.169*	.040
Constant	−14638.00	-2762.31	−16374.83	−6914.49
χ^2	189.77*	68.79*	54.15*	30.68*
N	3,217	3,252	3,260	3,260

Notes: Conditional Change Models estimated with Maximum Likelihood TOBIT regression

Coefficients shown are metric regression coefficients

* $p < .05$

Table C.2. *Effects of Marriage Dimensions on Giving and Loaning*

Independent Variable	Gifts to Relatives	Gifts to Nonrelatives	Loans to Relatives	Loans to Nonrelatives
	Dependent Variables			
	Time 2			
Sex ratio	4266.72*	−1284.12	6035.42*	−509.60
Family independence	2149.71*	−279.67	−1471.98	−2218.82*
Spouse dependency	−66.90	−126.53	526.21	56.99
No. of children	543.75*	−204.47	−667.90*	−351.42*
Yrs. married	39.29	−10.23	64.77	−32.82
	Time 1			
Sex ratio	4149.72*	1394.52	4543.41	8960.22*
Family independence	1100.63	730.17	1902.65	1065.45
Spouse dependency	−344.91	−130.04	−944.09	33.42
No. of children	−811.35	105.17	180.00	−421.84
Age[a]	−214.63*	−27.37	281.25*	178.05*
Dependent variable at time 1	.318*	.485*	.205*	.301*
Constant	−25681.11	−3366.17	−31051.86	−21598.31
χ^2	43.43*	10.14	58.10*	24.74*
N	1,469	1,476	1,476	1,478

Notes: Conditional Change Models estimated with Maximum Likelihood TOBIT regression.
Coefficients shown are metric regression coefficients.
Coefficients for years married in time 1 were dropped due to multicollinearity.
[a] Age is the residual of age regressed on other age-related variables in the equation.
* $p < .05$

References

Auten, Gerald, and Gabriel Rudney. 1989. "The Variability of the Charitable Giving by the Wealthy." In *Philanthropic Giving: Studies in Varieties and Goals*, ed. Richard Magat (pp. 72–91). New York: Oxford University Press.

Badinter, Elisabeth. 1992. *XY: On Masculine Identity*. Trans. Lydia Davis. New York: Columbia University Press.

Bailey, Beth L. 1988. *From Front Porch to Back Seat: Courtship in Twentieth-Century America*. Baltimore: Johns Hopkins University Press.

Bane, Mary Jo, and Paul Jargowsky. 1988. "The Links between Government Policy and Family Structure." In *The Changing American Family and Public Policy*, ed. A. Cherlin (pp. 219–61). Washington, DC: Urban Institute Press.

Becker, Gary S. 1981. *A Treatise on the Family*. Cambridge, MA: Harvard University Press.

Berk, Sarah Fenstermaker. 1985. *The Gender Factory*. New York: Plenum Press.

Bernard, Jesse. 1982. *The Future of Marriage*. 2nd ed. New Haven, CT: Yale University Press.

Bianchi, Suzanne. 1995. "Changing Economic Roles of Women and Men." In *State of the Union*, Vol. 1, ed. R. Farley (pp. 107–54). New York: Russell Sage Foundation.

Brines, Julie. 1993. "The Exchange Value of Housework." *Rationality and Society* 5:302–40.

———. 1994. "Economic Dependency, Gender, and the Division of Labor at Home." *American Journal of Sociology* 100(3): 652–88.

Brines, Julie, and Kara Joyner. 1993. "Ties that Bind: Principles of Stability in the Modern Union." Paper presented at the Annual Meeting of the Population Association of America, Cincinnati, April.

Brody, Elaine M. 1984. "Parent Care as a Normative Family Stress." *Gerontologist* 25(1): 19–29.

Bumpass, Larry L., and J. A. Sweet. 1989. "National Estimates of Cohabitation." *Demography* 26: 615–25.

Bumpass, Larry L., J. A. Sweet, and Teresa Castro Martin. 1990. "Changing Patterns of Remarriage." *Journal of Marriage and the Family* 52:747–56.

Caplow, Theodore. 1982 "Christmas Gifts and Kin Networks." *American Sociological Review* 47(3): 383–92.

Cherlin, Andrew. 1978. "Remarriage as an Incomplete Institution." *American Journal of Sociology* 83(5):634–50.

————. 1992. *Marriage, Divorce, and Remarriage* (revised). Cambridge, MA: Harvard University Press.

————. 1996. *Public and Private Families.* New York: McGraw Hill.

Chiswick, Barry R. 1991. "An Economic Analysis of Philanthropy." In *Contemporary Jewish Philanthropy in America,* eds. Barry A. Kosmin and Paul Ritterband (pp. 3–15). Savage, MD: Rowman and Littlefield.

Chodorow, Nancy. 1973. "Family Structure and Feminine Personality." In *Woman, Culture, and Society,* eds. M. Z. Rosaldo and L. Lamphere (pp. 67–88). Stanford, CA: Stanford University Press.

Coleman, James S. 1971. *The Adolescent Society: The Social Life of the Teenager and its Impact on Education.* New York: Free Press.

————. 1988. "Social Capital in the Creation of Human Capital." *American Journal of Sociology* 94:S95–S120.

Collins, Randall, and Scott Coltrane. 1991. *The Sociology of Marriage and the Family.* 3rd. ed. Chicago: Nelson-Hall.

Coombs, R. H. 1991. "Marital Status and Personal Well-Being: A Literature Review." *Family Relations* 40:97–102.

Cooney, Theresa M., and Peter Uhlenberg. 1992. "Support from Parents over the Life Course: The Adult Child's Perspective." *Social Forces* 71(Sept):63–84.

Coontz, Stephanie. 1992. *The Way We Never Were.* New York: Basic Books.

Crago, M. A. 1972. "Psychopathology in Married Couples." *Psychological Bulletin* 77:114–28.

Crum, R. M., J. E. Helzer, and J. C. Anthony. 1993. "Level of Education and Alcohol Abuse and Dependence in Adulthood: A Further Inquiry." *American Journal of Public Health* 83:830–37.

Durkheim, Emile. 1951. *Suicide: A Study in Sociology.* Trans. John A. Spaulding and George Simpson. New York: Free Press.

Duvall, Evelyn, and Brent C. Miller. 1985. *Marriage and Family Development.* 6th ed. New York: Harper and Row.

Ehrenreich, Barbara. 1983. *The Hearts of Men.* New York: Anchor Books.

Erikson, Erik. 1950. *Childhood and Society.* New York: Norton.

Ernster, V. L., S. T. Sacks, S. Selvin, and N. L. Petrakis. 1979. "Cancer Incidence by Marital Status: U.S. Third National Cancer Survey." *Journal of the National Cancer Institute* 63:567–85.

Farber, Bernard. 1964. *Family: Organization and Interaction.* San Francisco: Chandler Publishing.

Friedman, Meyer, and Ray Rosenman. 1974. *Type A Behavior and Your Heart.* New York: Knopf.

Fischer, Claude S. 1982. *To Dwell Among Friends.* Chicago: University of Chicago Press.

Gallup, Jr., George, and Jim Castelli. 1989. *The People's Religion: American Faith in the 90s.* New York: Macmillan.

Garfinkel, Irwin, and Sara McLanahan. 1986. *Single Mothers and their Children.* Washington, DC: Urban Institute Press.

General Social Surveys, 1972–1993 [machine-readable data file]. 1994. James A. Davis, Principal Investigator. Chicago: National Opinion Research Center.

Gilligan, Carol. 1982. *In a Different Voice: Psychological Theory and Women's Development.* Cambridge, MA: Harvard University Press.

Gilmore, David. 1990. *Manhood in the Making: Cultural Concepts in Masculinity.* New Haven, CT: Yale University Press.

Glenn, Norval. 1982. "Interreligious Marriage in the United States: Patterns and Recent Trends." *Journal of Marriage and the Family* 44(August):555–66.

Goffman, Erving. 1979. *Gender Advertisements.* Cambridge, MA: Harvard University Press.

Goldscheider, Frances, and Linda Waite. 1991. *New Families, No Families: The Transformation of the American Home.* Berkeley: University of California Press.

Goode, W. J. 1970. *World Revolution and Family Patterns.* New York: Free Press.

Gotlib, Ian H., and Scott B. McCabe. 1990. "Marriage and Psychopathology." In *The Psychology of Marriage: Basic Issues and Applications,* eds. Frank D. Fincham and Thomas N. Bradbury (pp. 226–57). New York: Guilford Press.

Gove, W., J. Grimm, S. Motz, and J. Thompson. 1973. "The Family Life Cycle—Internal Dynamics and Social Consequences." *Sociology and Social Research* 58:56–68.

Gove, Walter R., Michael Hughes, and Carolyn Briggs Style. 1983. "Does Marriage Have Positive Effects on the Psychological Well Being of the Individual?" *Journal of Health and Social Behavior* 24:122–31.

Greenson, Ralph R. 1968. "Dis-identifying from Mother: Its Special Importance for the Boy." *International Journal of Psycho-Analysis* 49:370.

Gregor, Thomas. 1985. *Anxious Pleasures: The Sexual Life of an Amazonian People.* Chicago: University of Chicago Press.

Hayes, Cheryl D., ed. 1987. *Risking the Future.* Washington, DC: National Academy of Sciences Press.

Heckman, James J. 1976. "The Common Structure of Statistical Models of Truncation, Sample Selection and Limited Dependent Variables and a Simple Estimator for such Models." *Annals of Economic and Social Measurement* 5(4):475–92.

Herdt, Gilbert H. 1981. *Guardians of the Flutes.* New York: McGraw-Hill.

Hochschild, Arlie, and Anne Machung. 1989. *The Second Shift.* New York: Viking Penguin.

Hodgkinson, Virginia A., and Murray S. Weitzman. 1990. *Giving and Volunteering in the United States.* Washington, DC: Independent Sector.

Hodgkinson, Virginia A., Murray S. Weitzman, and Arthur D. Kirsch. 1990. "From Commitment to Action: How Religious Involvement Affects Giving and Volunteering." In *Faith and Philanthropy in America: Exploring the Role of Religion in America's Voluntary Sector,* eds. Robert Wuthnow and Virginia Hodgkinson (Ch. 5). San Francisco: Jossey-Bass.

Hu, Yuanreng, and Noreen Goldman. 1990. "Mortality Differentials by Marital Status: An International Comparison." *Demography* 27(2):233–50.

Hudson, Liam, and Bernadine Jacot. 1991. *The Way Men Think.* New Haven, CT: Yale University Press.

Hughes, M., and W. R. Gove. 1981. "Living Alone, Social Integration, and Mental Health." *American Journal of Sociology* 87:48–74.

Hunter, James Davison. 1991. *Culture Wars: The Struggle to Define America.* New York: Basic.

Independent Sector. 1994. *Giving and Volunteering in the United States: Findings from a National Survey.* Washington, DC: Independent Sector.

————. 1996. Giving and Volunteering in the United States: Findings from a National Survey. Washington, DC: Independent Sector.

Janoski, Thomas, and John Wilson. 1995. "Pathways to Voluntarism: Family Socialization and Status Transmission Models." *Social Forces* 74 (2):271–92.

Kingston, Paul W., and Steven L. Nock. 1985. "Consequences of the Family Work Day." *Journal of Marriage and the Family* 47(August):619–29.

————. 1987. "Time Together among Dual-Earner Couples." *American Sociological Review* 52(June):391–400.

Kirchberg v. Feenstra, 450 U.S. 455, 101 S.Ct. 1195, 67 L.Ed.2d 428 [1981].

Krause, Harry D. 1995. *Family Law in a Nutshell.* Eagan, MN: West Publishing.

Kreuz, L. E., and R. M. Rose. 1972. "Assessment of Aggressive Behavior and Plasma Testosterone in a Young Criminal Population." *Psychosomatic Medicine* 34: 321–32.

Kreuz, L. E., R. M. Rose, and J. R. Jennings. 1972. "Suppression of Plasma Testosterone Levels and Psychological Stress." *Archives of General Psychiatry* 26: 479–82.

LaRossa, Ralph, and Maureen LaRossa. 1981. Transition to Parenthood: How Infants Change Families. Beverly Hills: Sage.

Laumann, E. O., John H. Gagnon, Robert T. Michael, and Stuart Michaels. 1994. *The Social Organization of Sexuality: Sexual Practices in the United States.* Chicago: University of Chicago Press.

Layne, N., and P. Whitehead. 1985. "Employment, Marital Status, and Alcohol Consumption in Young Canadian Men." *Journal of Studies on Alcohol* 48:528–40.

Levy, Frank. 1987. *Dollars and Dreams: The Changing American Income Distribution.* New York: Russell Sage Foundation.

Lillenfield, A. M., M. L. Levin, and J. J. Kessler. 1972. *Cancer in the United States.* Cambridge, MA: Harvard University Press.

Lynch, J. J. 1977. *The Medical Consequences of Loneliness.* New York: Basic Books.

Macklin, Eleanor D. 1983. "Nonmarital Heterosexual Cohabitation: An Overview." In *Contemporary Families and Alternative Lifestyles*, eds. E. D. Macklin and Roger H. Rubin. Beverly Hills, CA: Sage.

Malinowski, Bronislaw. 1964. "Parenthood, The Basis of Social Structure." In *The Family: Its Structure and Functions*, ed. R. L. Coser. New York: St. Martin's Press.

Marshall, Lorna. 1976. *The !Kung of Nyae.* Cambridge, MA: Harvard University Press.

McLanahan, Sara, and Lynne Casper. 1995. "Growing Diversity and Inequality in the American Family." In *State of the Union: American in the 1990's*, Vol. 2, ed. R. Farley (pp. 1–46). New York: Russell Sage.

McLanahan, Sara, and Gary Sandefur. 1994. *Growing up with a Single Parent: What Hurts, What Helps?* Cambridge, MA: Harvard University Press.

Metropolitan Life Insurance Company. 1957. "Mortality Lowest in the Married Population." *Statistical Bulletin* 58:4–7.

Mirowsky, John, and Catherine E. Ross. 1989. *Social Causes of Psychological Distress.* New York: Aldine deGruyter.

Modell, John. 1989. *Into One's Own: From Youth to Adulthood in the United States, 1920–1975.* Berkeley: University of California Press.

Morowitz, H. J. 1975. "Hiding in the Hammond Report." *Hospital Practice* (August).

National Health and Social Life Survey. [Machine-readable data file]. 1992. Edward O. Laumann, Principal Investigator.

National Center for Health Statistics. 1995. *Advance Report of Final Marriage Statistics, 1989 and 1990. Monthly Vital Statistics Report,* Vol. 43, No. 12. Hyattsville, MD: National Center for Health Statistics.

National Longitudinal Survey of Youth (NLSY) [machine-readable data file]. 1996. Columbus: Center for Human Resource Research, Ohio State University.

National Survey of Families and Households (NSFH) [machine-readable data file]. 1996. Larry Bumpass and James Sweet, Principal Investigators. Madison: Center for Demography and Ecology, University of Wisconsin-Madison.

Nock, Steven L. 1988. "The Symbolic Meaning of Childbearing." *Journal of Family Issues*-Dec:1241–62.

———. 1992. *Sociology of the Family.* 2nd ed. Englewood Cliffs, NJ: Prentice-Hall.

———. 1993. *The Costs of Privacy.* New York: Aldine deGruyter.

———. 1995a. " Commitment and Dependency in Marriage." *Journal of Marriage and the Family* 57(May):503–14.

———. 1995b. "A Comparison of Marriages and Cohabiting Relationships." *Journal of Family Issues* 16:53–76.

Nock, Steven L., and Paul Kingston. 1984 "The Family Work Day." *Journal of Marriage and the Family* 46 (May):333–44.

———. 1987. "Time Together among Dual-Earner Couples." *American Sociological Review* 52:391–400.

Nock, Steven L., and Peter H. Rossi. 1978. "Ascription versus Achievement in the Attribution of Family Social Status. *American Journal of Sociology* 84:565–90.

———. 1979. "Household Types and Social Standing." *Social Forces* 57 (4):1325–45.

O'Connell, Martin. 1991. "Late Expectations: Childbearing Patterns of American Women for the 1990's." U. S. Bureau of the Census. *Current Population Reports,* Series P-23 #176.

O'Donnell, William J., and David A. Jones. 1982. *The Law of Marriage and Marital Alternatives.* Lexington, MA: D. C. Heath.

O'Neill, Nina. 1977. *The Marriage Premise.* New York: Evans.

O'Neill, Nina, and George O'Neill. 1972. *Open Marriage.* New York: Evans.

Orr v. Orr, 440 U.S. 268, 99 S.Ct. 1102, 59 L.Ed.2d 306 [1979].

Parsons, Talcott, and Robert F. Bales. 1955. *Family Socialization and Interaction Process.* Glencoe, IL: Free Press.

Pearlin, L, and J. S. Johnson. 1977. " Marital Status, Life Strains, and Depression." *American Sociological Review* 42:704–15.

Pietropinto, Anthony, and Jacqueline Simenauer. 1979. *Husbands and Wives.* New York: New York Times Books.

Reissman, C. K., and N. Gerstel. 1985. "Marital Dissolution and Health: Do Males or Females Have Greater Risk?" *Social Science and Medicine* 20(6):627–35.

Robinson, John P. 1988. "Who's Doing the Housework?" *American Demographics* 12:24–28.

Rose, R. M., T. P. Gordon, and I.S. Bernstein. 1972. "Plasma Testosterone Levels in Male Rhesus Monkeys: Influences of Sexual and Social Stimuli." *Science* 178:643–68.

Rossi, Alice S., and Peter H. Rossi. 1990. *Of Human Bonding: Parent-Child Relations Across the Life Course.* New York: Aldine deGruyter.

Rothman, Ellen K. 1984. *Hands and Hearts: A History of Courtship in America.* Cambridge, MA: Harvard University Press.

Shelton, Beth. 1992. *Men, Women, and Time.* New York: Greenwood Press.

Skolnick, Arlene S. 1992. *The Intimate Environment.* 5th ed. New York: Harper Collins.

Smith, D. S. 1992. "The Meanings of Family: Household Changes and Continuity in the Mirror of the American Census." *Population and Development Review* 18:421–56.

Smith, J., Mercy, J., and J. Conn. 1988. "Marital Status and the Risk of Suicide." *American Journal of Public Health* 78(1):78–80.

Soldo, Beth J., and Martha S. Hill. 1993. "Intergenerational Transfers: Economic, Demographic, and Social Perspectives." In *Annual Review of Gerontology and Geriatrics,* Vol. 13, eds. George L. Maddox and M. Powell Laughton (pp. 187–216). New York: Springer Publishing Company.

Sorenson, Annemette, and Sara McLanahan. 1987. "Married Women's Economic Dependency, 1940–1980." *American Journal of Sociology* 93:659–87.

Spain, Daphne, and Suzanne Bianchi. 1996. *Balancing Act: Motherhood, Marriage, and Employment among American Women.* New York: Russell Sage Foundation.

Spencer, Paul. 1965. *The Samburu: A Study of Gerontocracy in a Nomadic Tribe.* Berkeley: University of California Press.

Stack, Steven. 1992. "Marriage, Family, Religion, and Suicide." In *Assessment and Prediction of Suicide,* ed. Ronald Maris (pp. 540–52). New York: Guilford Press.

Stanton v. Stanton 429 U.S. 7, 95 S.Ct. 1373, 43 L.Ed.2d 688[1975].

Stanton v. Stanton 421 U.S. 7 95 S.Ct. 1373, 43 L.Ed.2d 688 [1975].

Stoller, Robert. 1985. *Presentations of Gender.* New Haven, CT: Yale University Press.

Thompson, Linda. 1993. "Conceptualizing Gender in Marriage." *Journal of Marriage and the Family* 55:557–69.

Thompson, E., and Colela. 1992. "Cohabitation and Marital Stability: Quality or Commitment?" *Journal of Marriage and the Family* 54:255–67.

Thornton, Arland. 1988. "Cohabitation and Marriage in the 1980s." *Demography* 25:487–508.

Tolson, Andrew. 1977. *The Limits of Masculinity: Male Identity and the Liberated Woman.* New York: Harper and Row.

Turner, Ralph. 1970. *Family Interaction.* New York: Wiley.

U. S. Bureau of the Census. 1992a. "Marital Status and Living Arrangements: March 1992." *Current Population Reports,* Series P-20, No. 468.

———. 1992b. "Marriage, Divorce, and Remarriage in the 1990's." *Current Population Reports,* Series P-23, No. 180.

———. 1993a. "Fertility of American Women: June 1992." *Current Population Reports,* Series P-20, No. 470.

———. 1993b. *Money Income of Households, Families, and Persons in the United States: 1992.* CPS P-60, No. 184.

———. 1994. "Marital Status and Living Arrangements: March 1994." *Current Population Reports,* Series P-20, No. 484.

———. 1996a. "Household and Family Characteristics: March 1995." *Current Population Reports*, Series P-20, PPL-46 (Detailed Tables supplement).

———. 1996b. "Marital Status and Living Arrangements: March 1995 (Update)." *Current Population Reports*, Series P-20, No. 491.

Verbrugge, Lois M. 1979. "Marital Status and Health." *Journal of Marriage and the Family* 41:267–85.

Wadlington, Walter, and Monrad Paulsen. 1978. *Cases and Other Materials on Domestic Relations.* 3rd ed. Mineola, NY: Foundation Press.

Waite, Linda J. 1995. "Does Marriage Matter?" *Demography* 32:483–507.

Weber v. Aetna Casualty and Surety Company, 406 U.S. 165, 175 [1972].

Weitzman, Lenore. 1981. *The Marriage Contract.* New York: Free Press.

West, Candace, and Don H. Zimmerman. 1987. "Doing Gender." *Gender and Society* 1 (2):125–51.

Whyte, Martin King. 1990. *Dating, Mating, and Marriage.* Hawthorne, NY: Aldine deGruyter.

Wilenski, Harold. 1971. "The Moonlighter: A Product of Relative Deprivation." *Industrial Relations* 3:105–24.

Williams, John E., and Deborah L. Best. 1990. *Measuring Sex Stereotypes: A Multi-Nation Study.* Beverly Hills, CA: Sage Publications.

Winship, Christopher, and Larry Radbill. 1994. "Sampling Weights and Regression Analysis." *Sociological Methods and Research* 23: 230–57.

Wisconsin v. Yoder, 406 U.S. 205, 92 S.Ct. 1526, 32 L.Ed.2d 15 [1972].

Wuthnow, Robert. 1991. *Acts of Compassion: Caring for Others and Helping Ourselves.* Princeton, NJ: Princeton University Press.

Index